Hayley DiMarco and Michael DiMarco

Revell

a division of Baker Publishing Group
www.RevellBooks.com

Published by Revell
a division of Baker Publishing Group
P.O. Box 6287, Grand Rapids, MI 49516-6287

Printed in the United States of America

    Library of Congress Cataloging-in-Publication Data
DiMarco, Hayley.
      B4UD8—before you date : 7 things you need to
  know before your next date / Hayley DiMarco and
  Michael DiMarco
          p.   cm.
      ISBN 978-0-8007-3308-7 (pbk.)
      1. Single people—Conduct of life. 2. Dating
  (Social customs)—Religious aspects—Christianity.
  3. Marriage—Religious aspects—Christianity.
  I. DiMarco, Michael. II. Title.
  BV4596.S5D56 2009
  241'.6765—dc22   2008044883

Published in association with Yates & Yates, LLP, Literary
Agents, Orange, California.

Contents

Contents

Before *B4UD8*

Aka—The Intro

B4UD8 is designed to help you be ready for your next date, whether it's your first or your 500th. **B4UD8** is about honestly looking at why you want to date and if you're ready to date with a purpose. And it's about preparing yourself to be the best date a person can have and to have the best dating life you can have. **B4UD8** is for anyone who hopes to have a date tomorrow or ten years from tomorrow. Tonight? Let's reserve that for reading this book. Whether your next date will be the first date of your life or just the first one since you bought this book, **B4UD8** will help you be prepared not only for the event but also for the outcomes that may come your way.

This book isn't so much about who you date as much as it is about you. If you want to have good dates (or at least non-disastrous dates) then you need to start where your power lies. And your power lies in you. You can't control the other person. You can't make them like you or make them act a certain way. All you can do is be the best *you* you can be, and then see how the best you interacts with them. So **B4UD8**, let's take a look at your ideas of dating, the opposite sex, and yourself. Let's explore what you bring to a

Michael,

Check it out, just like the textbooks in school. Meaty stuff over there in the wide column, bonus content here in the skinny. Yes, a textbook on dating!

Hayley,

I don't know if snarky comments count as "bonus" content, but thanks for calling me skinny!

dating relationship and what stupid things you may have done or still might do on a date.

Think of this like spring training. You're gonna read some things that might shock you about yourself or even make you mad. You're gonna see some things in yourself that you didn't realize were there, and you're gonna read some things you didn't know about life. Whatever the case, take it all in. Figure out how it applies to your life and see if working on yourself and the way you date doesn't make the dating experience a whole lot better.

Before We Go Any Further

Okay, so we assume you're reading this book before, and not during, your next date. So with that in mind, let's do a little self-assessment of your current thoughts about dating, shall we?

Why do you want to date?

What are the dreams God has laid on your heart (outside of dating) that you want to see fulfilled?

What do you want to come out of your next dating relationship?

What, if anything, was bad about your past dating relationships?

Do you or your parents have any rules about dating? List them here:

Describe your last date (if you've had one) in one word.

Michael,

Yikes, a pop quiz already? Is this graded?

Hayley,

Um, the ring on your finger says not only did you pass this class, you already graduated. In fact, you're teaching the class today, knucklehead!

Michael,

Phew! BTW, I love your pet names for me, sweetie.

What's your biggest fear when it comes to dating?

What's the funnest part about going on a date?

What's the worst part about going on a date?

What part of you is most vulnerable when it comes to the opposite sex? Your body, your heart, or your mind?

Are you more romantic or practical?

Which lyric fits you best: "when I fall in love it will be forever" or "this love has taken its toll on me"?

When two people are dating they shouldn't be dating anyone else. *True False*

Girls should be able to ask guys out.
    True False

When I am dating someone they should be like a part of my family, going to all my family functions and stuff. *True False*

Rejection is too scary, so I won't ever ask anyone out. *True False*

I want to save myself for marriage.
    True False

The next person I date will be the one I marry. *True False Who Knows?*

As you read this book, think about your preconceptions of dating. Really take a look at your answers to questions like these. What view do you have of dating right now and how is it changing as you read through the book? Challenge your own ideas and ours, and figure out what best fits you.

The Dating Ritual

When it comes to dating there are a million ways to do it. You might have already tried a couple and failed or found one you liked and stuck with it. Or maybe you are just starting to think about hopefully one day having a date and you don't know what you think about the where's, how's, and why's. Whatever your dating history, you've come to the right place. **B4UD8** is about you and your future. It's about taking charge of your life and not just letting relationships happen to you. **B4UD8** is about preparing your heart and your mind to become close (but not too close) to another human being, and it's about learning when you are ready and how to best date with a purpose.

Since the beginning of time guys and girls have been finding each other, loving each other, and most often, leaving each other. Some relationships have been successful while others have started wars, ruined lives, and tormented souls. And that's just Paris Hilton. Dating is one of the most life-changing things you'll ever do, and so going into your next date with knowledge and understanding will increase your chances of finding happiness over heartache.

Dating can be one of the most exhilarating and amazing things you'll ever do. Your heart will feel like it wants to explode with happiness, your mind won't let you sleep because it will only want to think of Miss or Mr. Dreamy. Dating can be like putting on happy goggles. Suddenly everything will look more beautiful, colors will be more vibrant, and the world will look like a wonderful place to live. Dating can also be like a drug, and unfortunately, after a breakup, you can go through just as much pain as an addict going through withdrawals. The truth is that however quickly and passionately you started the relationship is how quickly and passionately it will more than likely end.

The truth is that most people date by accident. They let their eyes or their hormones do the thinking for them, and they dive in without a game plan or at least an idea of what they're gonna do when they've got some hard decisions in front of them. Accidental dating can be a rush. Lots of people blame their accidental dates on fate. Serendipity, they call it. And that might be the case, but typically, more horrible relationships start by accident than amazing ones. So why not decide ahead of time what your dating plans are? Why not be prepared for the serendipitous relationship?

Before we go there, let's take a look at how this whole dating thing got started in the first place.

Beware the dating rituals on the island of Tango Pango.

Modern Dating Rituals

Dating is a relatively new concept. In biblical days, marriage didn't have anything to do with romance and dating. It had to do with necessity, dowry, peace treaties, parents' decisions, and stuff like that. People got together out of necessity most of the time. And it pretty much worked; guys and girls needed each other to survive. One would work the fields and provide protection and shelter while the other ran the house, raised the kids, and managed things close to home. But then something changed.

Slowly people had less and less of a need to grow or kill their own food. The Industrial Revolution happened (dust off your history notes). Women started making money on their own, and life got easier. And as that happened, people found that they didn't need each other for survival as much anymore. So relationships became more about want than need, and people started to pick one another based on what they liked in a person instead of what they had to have to survive. Marriage became less about putting food on the table and raising babies and more about personal happiness and self-gratification. And dating became the most popular way of finding a mate.

People demanded the luxury of trying people out to see who made them the happiest. And happiness became the number one motivator for marriage instead of survival and multiplication. Or at least the *pursuit* of happiness became number one. Most people will just call that pursuing love. And since pursuing love can be such a rush, the next thing that happened in the evolution of dating is that dating itself became the goal or fulfilling activity in place of marriage. No longer was dating seen as just a way to find your mate. It became a pastime or lifestyle, something to do on Fridays and Saturdays. And with that idea came all kinds of complications.

Think about this idea for a sec. When dating started to be something people did for fun and not just for the purpose of finding "the one," something funny happened. Well, not funny ha-ha but funny odd. People started confusing each other. Everyone had different ideas and motives for why they were dating, and feelings started getting hurt. The full-time Playa perfected the part-time old school gigolo. Females that were once looked at as "loose women" were now described as "active" or "confident." No longer was it a simple matter of "do you love me and want to marry me or not?" All kinds of complications hit the scene: Do you like me or is this just a fling? Do you ever want to get married or are you just using me? Are we just friends or something more? Do you like me like I like you? Since we're living together, we're exclusive now, right? Will you raise this baby with me?

The thing is, when you date without the same goal as the person you are dating, you are in for a world of hurt. And that's why **B4UD8** might be just the ticket. There are so many different ideas about dating out there that wires can get crossed and relationships can be messier than they should be. If people are on the same page, at least they can cut down on potential heartache. So let's take a look at some dating styles from the past and the present.

B4U read on, take a look at the list here and circle the one you think right off the top of your head is your style or philosophy. Then read on and see if you're right.

Old School Dating
Buddy Dating

Group Dating

Hanging Out or Chill Dating

Open Dating (aka Buffet Dating)

Courtship

Arranged Dating

Mentored Dating (aka Yoda Dating)

The Date

Old School Dating. In the classic sense of the date, at least since the early twentieth century, the guy initiates things. He makes the first move. The old school method of first moves is the phone. The guy calls the girl on the phone to ask her if she would like to go out with him. When she says yes and the day arrives, the guy goes to the girl's house to pick her up, usually in a car, in which he then drives her to their date destination. The first destination is usually a restaurant, then to a movie or concert. The guy pays for everything during the classic date. This is probably because the date is a foreshadowing of things to come. In other words, traditionally the man has been the money maker in households; he's the provider guy, so he starts things out by showing how well he can provide. And traditionally, girls love it and guys feel good about being the hero, so the classic dating scenario makes sense. To show how well he can take care of her, the guy will also do things like help her out of her seat, open doors for her, and even carry her over puddles so her nice shoes won't get wet. Ah, chivalry! Anyway, at the end of the classic date, guy takes girl home and asks her if she'd like to do it again sometime.

She smiles and says she would love to. And on and on it goes.

In old school dating, the structure of the dating relationship might be the most straightforward. The main question that needs to be answered of the classical dater is for what purpose are they dating? Recreational? Matrimonial? The upside is that the guy has taken initiative and pursues the girl because he is interested in her and wants to find out if she likes him. He wants her for himself, as a girlfriend and maybe even a wife someday. In this scenario there is not much guessing about the interest of the guy; he might even make his intentions clear in what he says and does. This style makes life for the girl much easier, as you'll soon see. The relationship may not work out, but at least both of them know what the deal is. There isn't any guessing about what kind of relationship this is.

Buddy Dating. More recently, dating has "evolved," as some would say. Now things can be a little less obvious and formal. In fact, it can be almost impossible to know if you are dating someone or are just friends. In this scenario, two people of the opposite sex spend time together, they go out together with a group of friends, they go over to each other's houses to hang out. They might even call each other and chat for hours. But there is no formal dating relationship. No saying, "Would you like to go out sometime?" or "I really like you." The relationship "just happens." And the potential attraction is more concealed. The only thing either knows for sure is that they are

Michael *and* Hayley's Story

When we met we were living two thousand miles apart, one of us (Hayley) in Nashville and the other in Washington. It took the modern miracle of the World Wide Web for us to actually meet. But maybe that's just because we weren't paying attention. See, we were born less than one month apart, only sixty miles apart, and grew up going to some of the same places, but we never connected with each other. Even though we didn't meet till after we were thirty, technically we probably did meet when we were teenagers at a restaurant where Hayley was a frequent diner and Michael was a frequent busboy. We think about what it would have been like if we both had been ready to date with a godly purpose at the same time and did connect with each other then. What would have happened? How much would our lives be different now? But we didn't, and instead we grew from the experiences (and gnarly mistakes) of our individual lives and came together when we were ready for each other. Though we wish we would have married each other in or right after college, we are glad that we finally met when we did. We often think if we would have gotten our acts together sooner and learned the seven things in this book, God would have allowed us to meet sooner. In other words, we like to think our love was meant to be, we just wasted time and messed up a ton along the way.

friends. And at least one of the participants doesn't want to mess up the "friendship" to see if there is something more. Sometimes this arrangement organically evolves into a dating relationship, but many times it just stays stuck on friendship (for better or for worse).

In the modern buddy scenario there are a lot of unanswered questions. Does he like me? Does she like me? Is there more than friendship? Will we ever know? Will I feel jealous when the other person starts dating somebody else? And the questions go on and on. One of the biggest downfalls of this scenario is the inability to define the relationship and the potential for one person to like the other much, much more, which usually ends in a destroyed friendship, a broken heart, and an unreturned iPod. Though it's very easy to fall into this kind of relationship because you don't risk a lot at the beginning, you can risk much, much more in the end than in the classic dating scenario where things are more defined.

Group Dating. This is a really popular one. It requires little risk and makes it easy to be around someone you are digging without having to make it completely known to them. Group dating can be a safe way for, well, a group to hang out and keep each other from getting into emotionally or sexually dangerous situations. And group dating can be great fun, building strong relationships inside the group. If you have made your intentions known to the one you like but have chosen to date them only in a group, then you may have found a really safe alternative to the old school date. But not unlike buddy dating, group dating can leave some people confused and bewildered. If you haven't made your feelings known to each other and are just using the group to spend time together without making any moves to let your intentions be known, it can be super hard to know who likes who and can even start some tiffs when two girls like the same guy or vice versa. Group dating can be an ambiguous way to pursue someone, but it can also be a play-it-safe way to find out who is worth risking a real relationship for.

Chill Dating. One variation of friendship dating is hanging out. In a lot of relationships you

Michael,

Oh and remember when you were going to college and the volleyball team I played on was on your campus for tournaments a couple of years in a row?

Hayley,

I forgot about that! Remember, I still wasn't a Christian then. Hardly ready.

Michael,

Yeah, and I was a CINO—Christian In Name Only. Lot to learn about living with a purpose.

see around you in the twenty-first century, guys and girls "chill" together. In the chill situation, it's more than being "just friends" in the buddy scenario, but it's less formal than classic dating. It's obvious the two like each other, but there is no formal commitment to the dating process. The couple simply hangs out, a lot. They act like a couple, and they do everything together, but they say they aren't dating. In the chill model, things just happen. Everything is less formal and more laid back. That means, many times, that the couple is more laid back and less reserved in the physical aspect as well. They seem to be more focused on having a good time hanging and getting physical than dating with any kind of purpose.

In the chill scenario things are just as undefined as in buddy dating, but because things are so laid back, they can get a lot deeper a lot quicker. That means that couples that start out by just chilling can end up doing things sexually that other dating couples might more easily avoid. When there are no formal relationship boundaries, it can feel like there is a lot more freedom for both checking things out and exploring different options with both that person and other people. The chill method leaves you open for major heartache because of its lack of structure and definition.

Buffet Dating. Buffet dating (or open dating) is the way to have your cake and eat it too, or at least that's the hope. It's when two people consciously decide to date not only each other but other people too. Open dating says, "I think you are fun to hang out with and I'd like to date you for the time being. But when someone better, or at least as good as you, comes along I'm going to date them too. And you are free to do the same." We call it buffet dating because it's like eating at one of those big buffet restaurants; you might start at the salad bar, then move to the Chinese food bar, and then return for more salad. And no one should be offended if you sample and re-sample the different offerings until you're fat and happy. This open-ended way of dating is a way to date without any commitment or strings attached, but also with no real concern for the other person's feelings and a detaching from any personal responsibility for the consequences of your actions. Buffet dating is really just a chance to date mostly for fun, with an emphasis on volume. The theory being, the more people you date, the more chances at finding your one true love (or buffet food). That makes buffet dating a very dangerous game because there can be so many players. And you know how hard it is not to overeat when noshing at a buffet.

Mentored Dating Styles

There is another group of dating styles that is a little bit different (and maybe even more old-fashioned) and involves more than just two people. It's basically like hiring a consultant or mentor for your dating life. That's when it's you, your crush, and a third, wiser party who helps you make sense of the relationship and if it's a good fit. The third party can be a parent, pastor, or trusted advisor who serves as a kind of guard for your heart. Here are some of those types.

Courtship. Courtship (or really old school dating) is a growing trend in the church and has a vocal following. In courtship the guy usually starts things, like he does in old school dating, but instead of calling up the girl he calls up the girl's dad and asks for a sit-down. In this conversation the guy would tell the dad his intentions to court/date his daughter and ask his permission. This isn't a hard and fast rule; some couples find each other interesting, discuss courtship, and then involve the parents. The kicker here is that the pre-courtship convo with the parents usually talks about pursuing the girl for marriage. In courtship dating, the couple both know the intentions of one another and have the same goal at the outset. The involvement of the parents helps couples not go too far too fast, taps their wisdom in knowing their children and who's going to be a good match, and weeds out the recreational dating found in the other methods.

Courtship dating is great for kids who still live with their parents and whose parents have a solid faith, want the best for their kid, and consistently show good judgment in their lives and with their relationships (especially their marriage). One of the reasons this method works well with teens still at home is that the parents are still physically as well as emotionally responsible for their kids. They have total access to their kids, and so this form of dating can work well. For older singles who don't live at home anymore, courtship can be a little tougher, since your parents aren't where you are, and depending on how old you are they might not know you as well anymore. But that said, getting a wise and loving parent involved in helping you choose your mate is never a bad idea.

Yoda Dating. If a person doesn't have access to a parent or doesn't have a parent who has the same values as they do, they sometimes ask a trusted counselor, mentor, or Yoda to help them out. "Break your heart she will, hmmmmm." If you're like Luke and listen to wise counsel, this method saves you a lot of heartache. If you're more like Anakin, all that heavy breathing (through a scary black mask) will catch up with you. A pastor, wise friend, or other relative can be a great help when working through the hormonally charged areas of a relationship. In this dating scenario a guy and girl might ask the mentor (or Yoda) to help them work through their relationship questions and planning. It might be called premarital counseling or just **B4UD8** compatibility counseling from a friend. The couple choosing this option might date like the classic dater or the courtship daters; either way they involve a third party in their thinking.

Not every puppet is a certified B4UD8 counselor.

Arranged Marriage. Not to leave out the time-tested and oh-so-biblical technique for finding your future mate, let's talk about arranged marriages. In some cultures, arranged marriages are still the norm, but for most of us, this style of finding true love lacks that "I control my happiness" vibe. But in biblical days this was the way

The Love Boat?

Gather 'round, children, and let me tell you a story! There once was a young Italian man coming to America by boat to start a new life and family. He looked across the deck of the ship and saw a beautiful young woman with her family also traveling to the New World. As was the custom, he approached the girl's father and said, "My name is Eduardo, and I'd like to marry your daughter." The father looked Eduardo up and down, saw he had a strong back, and heard he was from a good family, so he said, "Let me introduce you to Louisa." Eduardo's excitement and anticipation left his face when the father brought him a slightly older and significantly stockier young woman to meet (also with a strong back). Eduardo said sheepishly, "I thought *she* was your daughter," pointing to the young woman he had first laid eyes on. The father said, "Oh, she is my daughter. But Louisa is my oldest, you can marry her." Eduardo looked Louisa up and down and uttered a barely positive "Eh" with a resigned shoulder shrug. The two were married until Eduardo's death at eighty-seven, and Louisa passed at the age of ninety-two. I just called them my grandparents!

things were done. Marriage wasn't about finding the perfect person; it was about a covenant between two people to live together and to help one another in life. As many arranged couples have said, "You learn to love each other." Arranged marriages generally put the marriage covenant in a more honorable and important place than individual feelings and desires, and that might be why many arranged marriages last longer. Of course, arranged marriages don't really allow for much dating, but no discussion of dating and its purpose would be complete without at least touching on the original way that couples came together. Think Adam and Eve!

Okay, so you've had a look at all the different ways you can date. Did any get your attention?

Did they change the way you see yourself dating? There are no hard and fast rules about dating, even for Christians. Some would say only one way is biblical, but if you take a look at the Bible you'll see no mention of dating at all. It didn't happen. God put men and women together in both simple and intricate ways, at the desire of singles' hearts and by the counsel or mandate of parents and mentors. And calling any of these methods more biblical than the other is like saying singing in the choir is more biblical than singing to God in the shower. There are no biblical commands on how to date, so choosing your dating method is totally up to you (and your parents if you are still living under their roof), but of course, some of these methods are more physically and emotionally risky than the others and can lead to *unbiblical* living, but we'll get into that later. There are all kinds of other biblical commands that can be applied to your dating life (like seeking wise counsel, fleeing sexual immorality, etc.), but they are the same commands that apply to your everyday life whether single or married, so the lesson here is be the same person you are when you are dating as you are at church or at home. Be consistent. Don't lead two different lives, one with your Christian friends and one with your love interest.

So now that we've covered some of the different ways you can dive into the dating pool, whether with water wings or off the high dive, let's talk about all the things (well, at least seven) you must know before you dive in again or even for the very first time.

1: Date with a Purpose

Okay, let's keep first things first (if you don't count the intro as first, and we're not, mm-kay?). **B4UD8**, let's make sure you have a good idea of the purpose of dating. Different people can have different purposes for the same activity. Some people think the purpose of dating is having a good time, getting out, and getting seen. Others think the purpose of dating is popularity or fitting in. And some think the purpose is to conquer as many people as possible. But there are still some holdouts, like us (and maybe you), who think that the purpose of dating is to find the person you want to spend the rest of your life with.

One thing you're gonna notice in **B4UD8** is that we want you to make up your own mind about things and always seek wise counsel before you act. We aren't going to give you some "you have to do this to be holy" kind of thing. And we aren't going to give you some kind of formula for finding "the one." But we are going to give you options along with the potential consequences of those options. An informed person making choices for themselves is much more likely to follow through on those choices than a person who is being told what to do. And that's why we won't tell you what to do. You might see that we lean this way or that, but our goal is to give you the scenarios as best we can and let you choose.

God lets you do the same thing. Ultimately you have to choose whether you do what he says or not. No one can make you holy. No one can order you to be faithful. Sure, someone can force you into obedience, but once you are no longer under that person's power, you can break away and do whatever you want. So before you rebel against anything or anyone, let's get some facts into your dome. Let's help you make choices that are the best for you as a follower of Christ.

Dating for Fun

Sometimes people date with only one goal. Fun. They really like the feeling of chasing or being chased. They love getting to know someone new and going fun places with a little hottie on their arm. In the harshest take, dating with no other purpose than having fun is a good choice for people who live for themselves. Dating for fun says life is about me and my enjoyment. It says I don't think about the future, excessive wear and tear on me, or breaking anyone's heart. I'm just concerned with getting the most out of my life. Now that can be both egotistical and educational, depending on who you are and how old you are. If you are twenty-six and still dating just for fun, then you have probably left a trail of destruction behind you. Because if you live your dating life with only the purpose of having some fun, then you've probably dated a few people who had different ideas on the purpose of dating. And chances are those people got hurt by your lack of concern or commitment. But listen, if you were only living for yourself, then you achieved your goal. A life with and for yourself alone. Okay, that kinda sounds cold and lonely, but hey, it's an option. Like licking a frozen metal pole is always an option.

Of course, if you are still in school and trying to figure out who you are and what you want, dating for fun might not be a bad thing. After all, if you aren't old enough to get married, then you aren't old enough to make the goal of dating to find a mate. And dating may be a good way to find out more about what kind of person you like and don't like. It's a way to explore life with the opposite sex. But that exploration can come with some danger zones. For example, the more you date, the more you break up. And the more you break up, the better you get at leaving someone. In other words, it's kinda like practicing divorce. And if you believe God's Word, then you already believe that divorce is a no-no. So why get that pattern ingrained in your psyche when it's, well, illegal according to God's law? That's why parents and mentors who allow dating for fun usually restrict it to group dates, where a group of guys and girls (not paired up) get to know each other but without the laser beam focus on one other person.

One of the big dangers of solo dating for fun is that when "fun" is your goal, you often will do whatever you have to do to achieve that goal. And that's what makes statistics like this one possible. Researchers* at Columbia and Yale Universities found that students pledging abstinence were just as likely to get STDs as students who didn't prom-

* (2005, researchers Peter Bearman, PhD, of Yale University, and Hannah Brückner, PhD, of Columbia University.)

ise abstinence. Good Christian kids who date for fun will do "fun" things with each other without even thinking if these things are covered under the term "abstinence." More on that later. So dating for fun has some major pitfalls.

Let's recap the pluses and minuses of dating for fun:

Pluses—fun, variety, learning what type of person you like before you are ready to get married, safer in group settings

Minuses—in solo dating scenarios: self-obsession, broken hearts, broken promises, sexual temptation, practicing divorce

Dating to Be Popular

Dating can serve many purposes, and one of them is pulling you up the social ladder. It's no secret that when you date someone everyone else likes, your value goes up in the crowd's eyes. Who you date can make or break your popularity. And so for some people, dating is just a way to get ahead. This concept has been around for decades. In the days of kings and queens, fathers would give their daughters to men for marriage so they could get more power or save their kingdom or stop a war. Coupling up with a certain someone sometimes has a weird effect on the social structure around you. And so dating can be just a tool to help a person get ahead. (Hello, K-Fed.)

The trouble with that approach is that it's pretty self-centered. When two people date there is almost always at least one heart involved. And using

Hayley,

For most of my life I dated for fun. When I was young I decided I didn't want to get married, so I just went out with guys for the thrill of it all. It was fun while it lasted, but now, looking back, I wish I hadn't done it that way. I spent ten years of my life just "having fun" and then had nothing to show for it. In other words, I had invested all this time and energy in short-term relationships. All I had left was a broken heart and a few fond memories of people I'd never see again. My life could have been so much better if I had stopped flitting from guy to guy and started to consider God's purpose in my life and the purpose of dating. Maybe I could have had all those memories with Michael instead of with guys I'll never see again.

someone to further your life position is like playing Russian roulette with their heart. It's a very me-centered dating style—duh! But trouble is, if this is your style, then you probably haven't stopped looking in the mirror long enough to see how self-obsessed you are. Harsh! Now, there are times when two people date like this with the same intentions. Like a Hollywood couple who only date so that they can get back on the cover of the tabloids. And then they break up for the same reasons. It's just business. But chances are your life is a little different than theirs, and a press release on your dating life isn't in your future. So if you think the purpose of dating is to help you fit in or gain power, then you have a few things to look forward to.

First of all, you can expect to become jaded. This means that love starts to mean nothing to you other than being a tool to build your image. You look at dating as a strategy, and love loses its luster. Over time, people who date for popularity's sake find themselves completely alone and wondering what happened to the good old days. Cuz popularity passes; just ask Michael Jackson. Shamon!

Second, people who date just to be popular burn a lot of bridges. If you have a hate club instead of a fan club of old crushes then look out, because your reputation might get in the way of finding true love one day. Play with people's hearts long enough and you'll eventually get what you give.

Finally, it's really hard to be a genuine human being and even harder, if not impossible, to follow Christ while using the dating relationship as a

Michael,

Dating for fun was almost non-existent in my life. I always fell too hard too fast. I always envied the guys who could do it. They seemed way more in control than I was. But I think we're going to see some better solutions somewhere in the middle. Let's keep going!

tool to achieve your selfish goal of being loved by your peers instead of God. Remember, if you are trying to please man you are no longer pleasing God (Galatians 1:10).

So let's recap, shall we?

> Pluses—popularity, climbing the social ladder, huge divorce settlements
>
> Minuses—self-obsession, becoming an approval junky instead of pleasing God, following the crowd instead of Christ

Dating to Conquer

She's just another notch on my belt. Have you ever heard someone say that? Neither have we since the eighties, but you know what we mean. It's the goal of someone who thinks the purpose of dating is to conquer as many people as possible. They just tally up the number of hearts they've broken like some giant scoreboard. Sure, they have fun flirting and fooling around with strangers, but ultimately their goal is the score.

Dating to conquer people doesn't need too much of an explanation. If you think that dating is just a way to get someone to like you so that you can prove you can get that person to like you and then move on to the next challenge, then you are dating to conquer. It's pretty hard to find any redeeming qualities to this kind of thinking. But finding some pitfalls shouldn't be too hard. Let's see, uhmmmm . . . Well, first of all it's arrogant, selfish, self-obsessed, heartless, manipulative, and unfair. You're a sexual and romantic glutton. You

Time Line	Hookup Lingo
Oldest	–"Just another scratch on the cave wall."
Fairly old	–"Just another mark on the bedpost."
	–"Just another notch on my belt."
Current	–"Just another hookup."
Future	–"Just another holopatch on my hoverbed."

leave a trail of broken hearts in your path, and this makes you a villain in the lives of all of your notches. But God loves you, so you've got that going for you. Guess that pretty much recaps it for this one. So let's move on, shall we?

Dating to Find the One for You

Dating is a good way to find out if someone is right for you or not, and so its purpose seems pretty clear for someone who hopes to one day find the one for them. If you want to be married someday, if you've decided that *alone* isn't your favorite word, and if you want someone to grow old with, make babies with, and have fun with for the rest of your life, you are probably interested in dating to find the one for you.

As we've said in the previous section, there are several ways to find your future mate, but all of them except one involve dating of some sort. So unless your parents are hand picking your future spouse for you and you are marrying them sight unseen (props, Gramps), then you are going on at least one date with your future "better half." Dating is by far the most popular way to find your love. And though there are other purposes for dating out there, its primary purpose for most God-fearing people is to find a mate. So let's dissect this even further. You see someone you think is cute. You would like to see if you "like them" like them, and so you watch them. You talk with them in passing. You hang out where they hang out and you see a spark between the two of you. But how do you interact when you are alone? Can you talk with each other? Can you get along? Do you like the same things? Have the same views on eschatology? (Google it.) These and many more questions can be answered by going on a few dates. Those dates then help you to decide if this person is a good fit for your mate, your love. Once you think they are, well, then time will tell. You spend time together, you laugh, you cry, you learn. And eventually you find out if it's love, hate, or something in between. If love is the outcome, then wedding bells may ring.

Like all other purposes of dating, this one can have its danger zones. If you are dating to find the one for you, your future husband or wife, then you better be ready to find that one. And when you find the one, you have to be ready to marry the one. Sounds great, huh? I mean, that's the goal. The trouble comes in when you aren't old enough to be marrïed or to even think about being married. If you are too young to buy the rings, get a home, pay for the car, and have a steady job, then you are too young to be thinking about who you are going to marry, and so dating can no longer be about that for you. OK, you can be *thinking* about it, but you shouldn't be on the dating market if this is your purpose and you aren't ready to get married. The question then is why are you dating? Go back and see if any of the other reasons sound good to you. If they don't fit who you are or who you want to be, then it's time to think about why you would date at all at this point in your life.

The other danger zone for dating to find the one is when finding the one becomes more important

Michael,

For us it was wedding seashells on a beach in the Bahamas. Or maybe wedding cruise ship horns. But I digress . . .

Hayley,

I love it when you digress. Combining our wedding and honeymoon trip was a stroke of genius!

than following your purpose in life. If there is something that you know you are destined to do, a calling on your life that you believe God has laid on your heart, you have to be very jealous about not letting anything or anyone distract you from that purpose. Dating can be one of the biggest distractions in anyone's life, especially when you put a lot of weight on finding the one for you. So it makes sense to get your priorities right **B4UD8**. While your head is clear, decide what your goal is and how you will get there and then beware not to let anyone derail you from that goal.

So let's recap:

Pluses—finding the one, honorable, dating path of least potential destruction

Minuses—too serious too soon, finding the one but being too young to do anything about it, getting distracted from your purpose in life

B4Ugo

Okay, so the first thing you need to know is what is your purpose for dating. Are you interested in fun or something more? Dating has a purpose, no matter who you are or what you think. It's up to you to decide what the purpose will be for you. Until you figure that out, it's probably best not to date at all, because no matter what anybody says, dating affects people's hearts. And it's a sad and dangerous thing to play with another's heart. God wants you to be kind and care about others, not risk their hearts for the

Michael,

When I was in college I was obsessed with finding the one. So when I knew I found her, I was super-stoked. But when her dad said I couldn't date her because I was "going nowhere," I dropped my plans to finish college and go to seminary and decided to get a "real job." I remember telling my college pastor that I had to make money so I could get the girl. Dating to find the one is a good purpose for dating, but when marriage becomes your obsession, you may lose track of your God-given purpose in life.

sake of your good time. Make sure you have an understanding of not only your purpose in dating but also the purpose of the person you are dating. The only way to limit the heartache is to make sure that everyone is on the same page. We aren't telling you to define the relationship on the first phone call, but find out about the life of the person you are dating. Do they date a lot? Have they had a long-term relationship? Do they have a reputation? You have to do the homework in order to protect your heart as well as theirs. So **B4UD8**, figure out the purpose of dating in your life and the lives of those you are crushing on.

Working Through It

After you read something, it's always good to think it over, let it soak in, and figure out how it applies to you. When you do that, let the Holy Spirit guide you. Let him talk it over with you. Put your heads together and make a plan for your life. Who can you use as a Yoda figure for trusted counsel? How will you date? Who will you date? And why will you date? To help you get started, here are a few things to ask yourself:

What's the purpose of dating, for you?

Which style of dating seems to make the most sense for you and/or your parents? Talk about this with them if they are making decisions for you. Find out the best way to go about finding the one for you and still get their blessing.

This is the elusive second date.

Here is an example of a date.

If you're gonna give up dating altogether, at least until you are ready to marry, then what are you going to do when the most amazing person in the world starts to show an interest in you B4UR ready?

What's your biggest weakness when it comes to the opposite sex?

How can you guard your heart so that you don't do something you know you don't want to do?

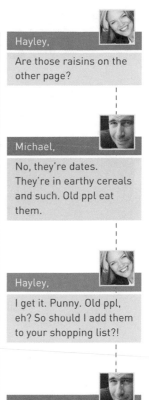

Hayley,

Are those raisins on the other page?

Michael,

No, they're dates. They're in earthy cereals and such. Old ppl eat them.

Hayley,

I get it. Punny. Old ppl, eh? So should I add them to your shopping list?!

Michael,

No, they would taste funny in my Apple Jacks.

Q4U | *from B4UD8.com*

My boyfriend is not as into the Christian thing as I am. He's getting there and he's not like completely against God and he's cooperating with me in getting there. Do you have any suggestions on how to help me get him closer to God?

Cassie

Dear Cassie,

Here's the deal: it's a really dangerous thing to date a nonbeliever. And if "not as into the Christian thing as I am" means he's not a believer, then you're playing with fire. As a Christian you cannot be with a non-Christian. It says in 2 Corinthians 6:14 that a believer and a nonbeliever cannot be hooked together, as in married. And since the ultimate purpose of dating is to decide if this is someone to marry or not, you already have your answer. He's not someone you are to marry, according to God's Word.

HD: I know how hard it is to love someone who doesn't love Jesus, but you have to stop. I've been in your shoes and I had to walk away from someone I loved, but God used that for good. I found, instead of the wrong guy, the perfect guy, by trusting God to bring him to me. Now I am so glad that I didn't compromise or try to pretend like being with someone who didn't love God was okay.

You cannot be with someone who doesn't love your God. That's a sin. It isn't your job to save him or disciple him either. He needs a guy who can do that. It isn't fair for you to be his discipler, there's too much passion or chemistry between the two of you for him to be honest in his faith. It's unrealistic to think that you can be the one to save him. Remember, that's not your job, it's God's. Your job is to obey God and to trust him to send you the right one for you.

Submit your Qs 4 us at B4UD8.com!

2: Take Care of the Temple

What's the Temple?

> Don't you know that you are God's temple and
> that God's Spirit lives in you? If anyone destroys
> God's temple, God will destroy him because God's
> temple is holy. You are that holy temple!
>
> 1 Corinthians 3:16–17

The second thing you need to know **B4UD8**
is that you've got to take care of the temple. If
you research the word *temple*, you will find that
a temple is the residence of a deity and/or a place
where that god is worshipped. It is something sa-
cred and holy and must be protected at all times.
The temple is almost as important as the god who
is in it, simply because that is the god's dwelling
place. When you become a Christian and the Holy
Spirit fills you, you instantly become a temple.
God lives in you, and so all the rules change.
Your body is no longer your own. And it probably
doesn't have to be said, but a temple is a very
important thing and not a place you throw your
trash around or where you throw wild parties.

So how good have you been at taking care of
the temple? Is there something that you've done
to your body that you now regret? Is your temple
squeaky clean or a little dusty and scratched up?
Is it falling apart or is it beautiful and well kept?

B4UD8, it's important to understand the role you and your body play not only in your dating life but also in your spiritual life. Taking care of the temple not only helps you become closer to God but also can positively affect your dating life as well. No matter what condition your temple is in right now, there is still time to take care of it.

Cleaning Up the Temple B4UD8

There is a lot involved in taking care of a temple; just ask the janitor at your church. Taking care of a temple is a full-time job, and it's no different when it comes to your body. Both the inside and the outside of the temple have to be cared for. Why? Well for one, because it's the house of God. And who wants to live in a run-down, beat-up, ugly old house? And second, because if you take care of the temple, you're much more likely to attract the opposite sex. So let's look at how you care for your temple.

The Outside

B4UD8 it's important to take a look at the outside of your temple. A temple that is well cared for and loved looks like it. When people care about their temple they clean it, repair it, and guard it. They don't let it get run down or neglected. They wash the windows, pick the weeds, and vacuum the floors. A temple that is cared for is not only an honor to the God who lives in it but also an attraction to anyone who might be looking at it.

It's like this. Why is it that you can drive past a dilapidated old falling apart church and say "I'm not gonna even try that church. It looks like no one even goes there." But then you drive by a well-landscaped, clean church and say "I might try that one because it's beautiful. It looks like the people that go there take care of what God's given them." It's because you can clearly see from the street that the church family and staff care about that temple. They make an effort to be presentable and attractive to anyone driving by. They know that the temple is not theirs, but God's, and that they must be good caretakers of what God has entrusted to them. Now, that old, broken-down church might have a sweet group of believers that go to it. But it won't bring in new believers because that inner sweetness can't be seen from the road. It looks depressing or like the members and staff just don't care. When people see the weeds in the yard and the paint flaking off, they are turned off. And the same is true for your body. **B4UD8**, you've got to take a look at the temple from the outside and see what kind of a message you are sending. Are you falling apart, in disrepair? Or are you taking care of your temple? Cleaning it, caring for it, keeping it fit and healthy? No matter what you say, people decide what to think about you by how you look on the outside. You might be the most amazing person on the inside, but if people can't get past your falling-down exterior, then it's going to be tougher to see the sweetness inside you. So **B4UD8**, get to work on your outside.

Taking care of the outside of the temple means simple stuff like taking a shower every day. It means brushing and trimming your hair, cleaning your face, putting on deodorant. It means looking in the mirror when you get dressed and actually caring about how you look. Not obsessing but giving it some thought and some care. You don't have to do this if you don't want to. You can just say "take me as I am, love me or leave me." But good luck with that. People aren't usually attracted to falling-down and uncared-for buildings, and they aren't attracted to disheveled, stinky people who seem not to care about how they look (we're looking at you, McStinky).

Look around at the attractive people you see and you're gonna notice something. The attractive people are the people who care about eating right, being neat and clean, and taking good care of the temple. They don't let the natural decline get out of control. They manage themselves. They control their appetite and exercise routines so that they can look their best. And it pays off. People are attracted to other people who seem to give a rip. The good news is that doesn't mean you have to be naturally beautiful to get attention and attract the opposite sex, it just means you have to take care of the temple. Dust if off, clean it up, and dress it neatly. And suddenly your attraction level goes up.

Have you ever seen the show *Beauty and the Geek*? They take twelve geeky guys and twelve beautiful girls and put them together in a reality show. The guys look awful when you first see them. Geeky glasses, knee-high socks with shorts,

Pop quiz! Beauty or geek?

silly T-shirts, freaky hairstyles. They are anything but attractive. And the girls squirm. Yes, the girls are shallow, but by the end of the show the guys look different. The girls spend time with these guys that they otherwise would never have given the time of day to, and they get a chance to see their sweet interiors. And they learn to like them; some even fall in love with them. Amazing. But not only does this show help the girls learn to see beauty in geekiness, it also helps the geeks learn to present their inner good looks more accurately. They learn how to communicate with the opposite sex, they learn how to relax and have a good time, and they learn how to present themselves better on the outside. They get haircuts, facial cleansings, new clothes, and whamo! Suddenly the edge is taken off and the former geeks look like guys pretty girls would actually sit down with and talk to. It's an amazing transformation. And it just shows how important it is to care for the temple not only on the inside but on the outside.

Okay, this might sound shallow and all, but it's just common sense that you probably already knew. **B4UD8**, you've got to see yourself how others see you and then decide how you can improve yourself in order to get them to see you the way you want to be seen. That might mean a wardrobe change or a haircut. It might be a membership at the gym or a change in your diet. Who's up for a full back waxing? (jk) Whatever it is, taking care of the temple will only make a better package for your future love.

So here are some specifics you can think about if you want to make some changes to how you care for the temple.

Sending the Wrong Message

Everyone, whether they know it or not, has a marketing campaign, an image, that other people see and understand to be you. This means that every day that you walk out of the house, your choice of how you clothe yourself impacts how people treat you and think of you. That gives you a lot of power. You can help people know what to think about you by how you cover yourself. So take a look and see if your look clicks with who you are on the inside. Don't send mixed signals. Get a complete and accurate image of who you are, and that way **B4UD8** you'll be ready to find just the right person for you.

Body Out of Control

The sin of gluttony is essentially taking more than you need. How many days a week do you eat more than you need? Do you even know how much you need? If you aren't sure of the answer to that, then find out. Get onto www.mypyramid.gov and find out about eating. Talk to a counselor or other professional who understands nutrition and make an effort to take care of the temple better than you ever have before. If you know you have a problem with weight, think about eating as your act of worship. And do it only to feed the body what the body needs. The temple of God cannot be neglected or stuffed till it wants to burst and be truly cared for. Many illnesses result from overeating. And that's not caring for your temple. So make caring for God's house more important than satisfying your cravings and you might just find that not only does your relationship with God improve, but so do your relationships with others. **B4UD8**, you have to get control of your body and refuse to be a slave to anyone other than to God, even to your stomach or taste buds.

Tired of Being One of the Guys

This one is for girls who are tired of being thought of as "one of the guys." There are a couple of reasons this might be happening, but one of them could be the way you choose to dress. If you aren't caring for the temple when you get dressed but caring for your need for comfort, then you might be sending a signal that gets translated as "I'm not a girl who wants a guy to date. I'm a girl who wants guys as friends only." That probably isn't your true intention, but that's what it looks like from the outside. So if you are wearing baggy sweats, basketball shorts, and other "comfortable" clothes, then you might want to change your idea of apparel in order to catch the eye of boys. It's like the church building that is falling apart. If you dress like a slob, then guys who drive by think you don't care about attracting them and decide you must be "one of the guys" and off limits for dating. So **B4UD8**, think about how you present yourself by what you wear, and you might just find yourself no longer a buddy but a girlfriend, or at least a sought-after girl.

> **Michael,**
>
> I know I have to constantly fight the bad habits of eating when I'm bored or stressed. Food as a comfort drug trashes the temple. Or at least expands the walls in a marshmallowy sort of way.

> **Hayley,**
>
> I'd reply to this, but I'd have to put down my tub of ice cream . . .

Done with Being Ignored by the Girls

Just like the geeks on *Beauty and the Geek*, you want to be noticed. You are tired of being ignored. Well, we've got good news. Girls can be visual creatures too, especially when it comes to clothes. Most girls love everything that has to do with clothes, shopping, and fashion. So when you walk around looking like an explosion at the church lost and found, why are you surprised they don't give you the time of day? **B4UD8** you're gonna have to get some help. Talk to someone who gets it. Ask your sister or another female who you trust to bring you from geek to dude (when you walk by the girls, they shriek, "DUDE!"). It might seem shallow and ungodly, but just remember that you are a temple of an all-powerful God. And after all, you probably want an attractive, well-kept lady temple of your own, so why not "love others as yourself" and get to dressing well? **B4UD8** you have to stop making your fashion statement about you and your comfort level and start making it about honoring God and giving girls something visual to be interested in.

Obsessed with Clothes

For some of you, clothes are your obsession, and you have no problem looking good. But it's important to check yourself for the other extreme. If all you care about is your outside, how clean and shiny you look, how trendy and hot, then look out, because it's the same kind of story. People can tell a lot about your interior motives by looking at your exterior. And if your exterior seems to be your all-consuming passion, then it becomes pretty clear that the inside might just be neglected. So **B4UD8**, think about what interior decorating God wants you to do inside your temple and balance taking care of both the exterior and the interior. After all, God would rather have you obsessed with him and loving others than with yourself and your wardrobe. Don't let something as trivial as clothes take the position that God should have in your life.

> Listen to me, you Levites! Purify yourselves, and purify the Temple of the Lord, the God of your ancestors. Remove all the defiled things from the sanctuary.
>
> 2 Chronicles 29:5 NLT

Hayley,

Shoes aren't clothes right? RIGHT?!

Michael,

Ma'am, back away from the closet, we're here to help.

The Inside

No discussion of the temple would be complete without talking about the inside. Without taking care of the inside, you're just like one of those Old West movie sets where the buildings look authentic on the outside but on the inside it's just sticks holding up the outside wall. After all, the inside is where the Holy Spirit himself lives. It's where everything gets started, and it's an important part of temple care. The inside of your temple is stuff like your heart, your mind, and your spirit. And out of those three places is where all your bad traits and good traits get their start. So taking care of the temple means taking a look at your heart, your thoughts, and your spirit.

Heart

Let's take a look at the heart of the temple. This is where everything passes, and where a lot of things dig in and live. As it says in Proverbs, "Guard your heart more than anything else, because the source of your life flows from it" (Prov. 4:23). **B4UD8**, realize the importance of protecting your heart. Most of the time your body will follow wherever your heart leads, just like a lovesick puppy. And that's why it's so important to protect your heart. If you have your heart set on something, more than likely you're gonna do it, or at least not stop thinking about it till you do. That's why people say things like "put your heart into it." Or "she's got a lot of heart." The heart is like the quarterback of our life. Our heart directs how we move down the field. Run, pass, or take a knee. And so like a quarterback who's protected by his offensive line, you have to make a plan to protect your heart from getting bumped around. That doesn't mean you vow never to fall in love or avoid people altogether just to be safe. It means that you get smart and don't let your heart get ahold of stupid ideas. You don't encourage it to fantasize about sinful stuff. You don't let it fall in love on a whim, or be in a relationship with someone you shouldn't be sharing your heart with. So let's get to recruiting a bunch of 300+ pound guys to protect the pocket.

Hayley,

Girls, that's a football reference. Those big lineman protecting the QB form a "pocket."

Michael,

That's why you're my dream woman . . .

Heart Protection

In order to take care of your heart you're gonna need to know a few things. And these are them:

1. Know that your current (or next) crush is not "the one" until you both say "I do." That means if the one you are dating breaks up with you, it isn't the end of the world. There will be more. If you lie to yourself and believe they were the only one, then you risk making your pain last longer and feel worse. A clear perspective on "soul mates" can save you from wrecking your temple. No one is a "soul mate" until you've exchanged rings and vows and smashed cake into each other's faces A jilted lover will have no need to consider "ending it all" when they haven't bought the lie that they cannot live without this particular person.

Which leads to #2.

2. There is no one person you cannot live without. The heart is good at adding drama to your life. This drama manifests itself in the form of hyperbole, exaggerations, and little white lies. When it lies it tells you things like "I just can't live without this person." But the truth is that you can't live without food and water but you can live without a particular person in your life. Living shouldn't be about which person loves you or not but about the God who loves you. Keep your focus on him and you will be able to stand all the pressures of unrequited or jilted love.

3. Love can hurt, but it's worth it. Sometimes if you've been hurt by someone you loved, it can be hard for your heart to risk itself again. It will lie to you and tell you things like "love isn't worth it" and "I don't need anyone to be happy." A wounded heart can come up with all kinds of ways that it thinks are protecting you, but the truth

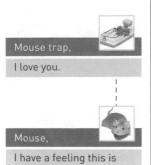

Mouse trap,

I love you.

Mouse,

I have a feeling this is going to hurt.

is that a heart that has a brick wall built up around it is a heart that is lying to you. It pretends that protection is king over all else. Everyone has seen a game where the QB gets hit right as he completes a long touchdown pass. Score! If that QB was all about his safety, he would have taken a knee just to avoid the hit. But the fact that he stood there and risked getting hit let his team put points on the board. Sometimes we start to let protection become a prison, and even a god. If anything, even protecting your heart, becomes more important than listening to God and loving others, then you've made that thing an idol. And idolatry is a dangerous thing. Don't let your hurting heart convince you to stop loving, because God calls us all to love everyone, even those who have hurt us.

> But I tell you this: Love your enemies, and pray for those who persecute you!
>
> Matthew 5:44

4. Love doesn't ask you to break God's law. B4UD8, it's important for you to learn that love never asks you to break God's law. If anyone ever says, "If you loved me you would . . ." and then some kind of sinful act comes next, then your heart needs to know immediately that this isn't love. Train your heart in God's Word and help it to know without hesitation what's sin and what's love. **B4UD8**, get to know God's law and have it written on your heart so that you know if anything anyone asks you is disobedience to God. And then be willing to say no and walk away from anyone confusing love with sin.

5. God works everything together for the good of those who love him. If your heart can learn this truth and truly believe it then you will have much success when it comes to dating. A heart that truly knows and lives these words is a wise heart that will rarely lead you astray. So keep these words close to your heart. Memorize them and never let them go.

> We know that all things work together for the good of those who love God —those whom he has called according to his plan.
>
> Romans 8:28

Protecting your heart from getting you off course and out of focus will save you from having to pick up its pieces later on. If the main goal of your heart is to find love, then chances are your heart is going to break and break hard very soon. But if the main goal of your heart is to know God and to do what he says, then you're gonna save yourself a lot of heartache. And in the end find a love that will endure.

Mind

The heart and mind are closely linked. It's like they live in the same duplex. In fact, some might say they function in the same way. But for this exercise we're talking about your thoughts. If your heart is set on something, then you are probably thinking about it. But your thoughts can also be at odds with your heart. For example, when in your heart you really, really want to kiss someone but in your mind you say, "They don't even know me so how could I walk up and kiss them right here in the mall?" Luckily, your mind can keep your heart from acting on some of the stupid stuff it comes up with. So when it comes to protecting the temple, you've got to make sure you protect your mind as well.

So let's start with a few Qs.

What kinds of things do you think about most of the day?

What would you say you think about the most?

How many times a day do you think about your crush?

It might seem like no biggie that you are thinking about doing things with someone that you know you'd never *really* do. In fact, you might be thinking about things that border on downright sinful. So what's so wrong with that? What does that have to do with protecting the temple? If you never do what you're thinking, then no harm no foul, right? Oops! Think again. Jesus said he's listening to your thoughts and they do matter, they matter as much as if you did exactly what you were thinking.

> You have heard that it was said, "Never commit adultery." But I can guarantee that whoever looks with lust at a woman has already committed adultery in his heart.
>
> Matthew 5:27–28

Did you catch that? If a dude just thinks about doing something with a chiquita, it's like he's already done it. Bam, and there's the temple, invaded and overtaken by the archenemy sin. Ugh-a-lee! Your thoughts have so much power. And that power can be used for good or for bad. You just have to remember that thinking about doing something bad but not doing it is just as bad as doing it, according to God. That means you have to stop the stuff before you start dreaming about it. **B4UD8**, you have to get control of your mind. Don't allow it to wander into dangerous territory. Stay focused. If you aren't strong enough to control your thoughts, then get to work, because until you can control your mind a little better, you best not be dating.

Mind Control

Finally, brothers and sisters, keep your thoughts on whatever is right or deserves praise: things that are true, honorable, fair, pure, acceptable, or commendable. Practice what you've learned and received from me, what you heard and saw me do. Then the God who gives this peace will be with you.

Philippians 4:8–9

So if you are ready to start taking better care of your mind, here are a few things you'll want to learn:

1. Clean up your dirty mind. Jesus made it clear that your thoughts count. And when it comes to the opposite sex, your thoughts matter to God. **B4UD8** you'll have to learn to control what you let your mind think about. The temple can easily get trashed if you let your mind concentrate on sinful stuff. You might not ever actually do anything, but that's irrelevant to God. In order to keep the temple clean you have to make up your mind not to think about or look at trash. That means staying away from anything that even gets you thinking about sex, fooling around, or even obsessing over romance. If there is anything that you fantasize about that makes you envy what you don't have or regret what you do have, you must stop. If there is anything that you look at or do that makes you depressed, resentful, lonely, or bitter, then don't look at it or think about it anymore. Keeping the temple clean includes keeping your thoughts on things that are godly, good, and positive. Don't let your mind wander off into sinful land and you'll start to see a big difference in the condition of your temple.

This is your brain on dirt. Any questions?

2. If you doubt it, don't do it. B4UD8, it's important to get it in your head that if you are thinking about doing something and you aren't totally sure it's okay, then don't do it. Because Romans 14:23 says that "if you do anything you believe is not right, you are sinning." So the best way to keep the temple clean is to avoid anything you aren't totally sure of. Your mind needs some help when it comes to protecting the temple. So find out what pleases God. Get to know his Word so that you don't risk messing up or diving in where you are uncertain. And always remember, if you're not sure if God wants you to do something you are thinking of doing, then err on the side of safety and don't do it.

3. You are what you think. In Proverbs it says about man "for as he thinks in his heart, so is he" (23:7 NKJV). That means you are what you think. If you think about overeating, then you are a glutton. Make sure that what you spend your time thinking about is consistent with what you believe about God and your relationship with him. **B4UD8**, it's important to know what you believe and to look at your thought life. Are you living in your mind what you believe in your heart? If there is a conflict within you, then you aren't ready to date.

4. Have an escape plan. In the heat of the moment it can be really hard to think straight. Your mind can get all fuzzy and confused and your heart wants to take over. Suddenly what looked wrong suddenly feels right, and your mind starts to play tricks on you. That's when the trouble hits. So before you get into trouble it's important to work things out. That means having an escape plan. Think about the pits you might fall into and then decide, while you have your wits about you, what you'll do to get out, to stop the action that's leading you to trouble. In the heat of the moment you'll be in a weakened state, and so having a solid "to do" plan that you've memorized will help you avoid trouble. Talk to your parents, your counselor, or your pastor. Come up with some ideas of ways you can get away from dangerous or risky situations before they ever even come up. Preparation is the best way to assure that **B4UD8** you are ready for anything.

Your mind is an important part of the temple that you are in charge of taking care of. In fact, your mind is the logic center for the entire temple. **B4UD8**, it's important to take an inventory of your daily thoughts, see how they match your beliefs and purpose, then decide if there needs to be some kind of change in order to take better care of the temple of the Holy Spirit.

Spirit

Protecting the temple is a big job. It's more than washing your hair and flossing your teeth. It's about not letting anything that's considered sinful in your mind, on your body, or in your thoughts. When you learn to protect the temple, you will be one step closer to being ready to date. But until then it's time to do the work you've got to do to get the temple and all of its parts secured and protected. And all that work starts with your own spirit. Inside your temple is not only the Holy Spirit but your spirit as well.

The Bod

B4UD8 it's important to get control of your body, your heart, your mind, and your spirit. All the things that are involved in any relationship, be it with another person or with your God. Dating without taking care of all that stuff is a recipe for disaster. Because if you date before you take care of the temple, you open yourself up to all kinds of idols that will want to take the place of God in your temple. When you get your temple under the control of the Holy Spirit, then you will be much better at loving and being loved.

One of the biggest ways to mess up and trash the temple is by starting down the slippery slope of getting physical. You've heard it all a million times. You've probably seen the videos: STDs and you. You know that premarital sex is not only dangerous but a sin. But have you ever thought about it like this?

Let's say you want to go out and buy a new car. You've gotten a gift of cash that will buy you any car you want. Are you gonna rush right out to the used car lot and look for a beat-up used car at a new car price? Just think about it for a minute. You see this old beater car, scratched up, dented, with high miles on it and a price just like the one on that new BMW. Would you say, "Oh wow, what a great deal! I'll take it." Probably not. Sounds like a stupid way to spend your money, huh? Well, what do you think happens when you start fooling around with someone you aren't married to? You start off just holding hands, maybe kissing a bit. But soon you want more. And more and more gets easier and easier, and each "more" adds more miles and more dings to your body. The more miles you put on yourself, so to speak, the less valuable you become to others. You start to get worn out and used up, and it shows. The temple looks run down, dirty, and empty. Suddenly you are no longer a beacon in the dark for lost souls but a dusty old lamp stuck in the corner, begging for someone to turn it on.

Easy financing! OK, just easy.

B4Ugo

If you are a Christian and you have the Holy Spirit living in you then you must understand

Michael,

I love old muscle cars from the 60s, but most of them are trashed. But you know what? With time and effort, they can be restored and become extremely valuable to the next owner. So the sooner you start the restoration, the more time the next owner will be able to spend honoring and cherishing!

that your body is a dwelling place for God. And because of that it is no longer your own and must be cared for and respected as a precious residence of the Father. When it comes to taking care of the temple you have to think about it from several different angles. Your heart, your mind, your spirit, and your body are all a part of the temple. If you let any of these areas go, you are neglecting God's holy temple and trashing his home. It's your turn to decide: will you believe God and trust his Word when he calls you his temple, or do you find that hard to believe? If you have a hard time controlling yourself and managing your body or your mind then you're probably not taking God at his Word. Don't let disbelief be your guide. Faith isn't a feeling, and that means you can make the choice right now to believe. You don't have to feel his presence or feel like a temple in order to believe. You just have to choose. So no matter what you have done to the temple in the past, it's time to clean up. Don't let yourself get run down, beat up, cut up, or burned out. Forget about yourself just for a minute and look at the temple for what it is, God's very own pad. Then choose to show him the respect he deserves. When you do, you will find all kinds of freedom from the things that control you. Choose not to be controlled by anything but your loving God. **B4UD8**, get the temple under control and vow to keep it that way.

Working Through It

Now, before you go on to the next chapter, let's work through what you've just read:

After reading this chapter what do you think are the parts of the temple you struggle with the most?

Exterior: fashion, weight, hygiene?

Interior: heart, mind, spirit, body?

What are three things you believe you need to do, based on this chapter, **B4UD8**?

There are lots of ways to protect the temple from invasion. Can you think of some ways that you can be prepared so that your temple stays clear of anything that isn't from God?

Are there any things you do that on the surface aren't sinful but because of how you think about them, overdo them, or idolize them they've got to go?

What does it mean that "your soul mate is the one you say 'I do' to"?

How does that make you feel about the argument of people who divorce because they didn't marry "the one"?

Read Romans 8:28. How could this apply to marriage?

Why do you think God forbids divorce?

List three reasons why taking care of the temple will be good for you.

Q4U | *from B4UD8.com*

I know this doesn't sound like a dating question, but I have a problem with my weight. I keep trying to lose weight but I can't seem to control myself. My life is out of hand, and when I stress I eat. My mom tells me to just stop eating so often, but I need the food to make my life bearable. How can I help her to understand that the food is the only thing good in my life right now?

Blake

Dear Blake,

What you are saying isn't some strange or unusual thing. It happens every day and all over the place—people using food as a comforter and hope and a way to find peace in their life. But if you notice, all those descriptions of food are also descriptions of God. In fact, God wants to be all the comfort, hope, and peace that we need. And believe it or not, he is. See, it's a lie to believe that you can't make it through the rough times without eating whatever you want. Food, when treated like your salvation in hard times, becomes an idol. A little god that you worship in order to get comfort. God is completely against rivals. "Never worship them or serve them, because I, the LORD your God, am a God who does not tolerate rivals" (Ex 20:5). He commands us all to have no idols and no gods other than him (Deut 5:7). Controlling your eating habits can become a spiritual endeavor when you think of it like this. And that's a good thing, but God has promised to help you. He has given you his Holy Spirit, and when you can look at things from a spiritual instead of an earthly perspective, you can find a greater strength.

The thing you have to do is call food what it is, your idol. Then decide to no longer betray your God by loving other idols. Ask God for help to do that and then determine to be faithful. This isn't just a matter of your waistline or your pants size but a matter of spiritual importance. "For of this you can be sure: No immoral, impure or greedy person—such a man is an idolater—has any inheritance in the kingdom of Christ and of God" (Eph 5:5 NIV).

MD: I know for a fact that food has been my idol. I have spent most of my life living to eat. I have found myself making it through the day by dreaming of what I would eat when I got home. It took years for me to realize that I was making food my god. For someone who loves food, I find it's a daily battle not to worship the stuff I eat. But the more you concentrate on God instead of a donut, the healthier and happier you become. So know that you've got a big brother on your journey of leaving that little god of food behind, and we'll stop living to eat and start eating to live.

For moral support on any B4UD8 topic you're working on, jump onto B4UD8.com or iFuse.com.

3: Dating Is Not Marriage

The third thing you need to know **B4UD8** is that dating is not marriage. Seems like a no-brainer, but is it? Before we go on, let's take a little quiz. Should be easy, so no sweat, here goes:

A man and a woman say good-bye after they go out. She goes to her house and he goes to his. *Dating, Married, or Both?*

A man and a woman share one bank account and make all financial decisions together. *Dating, Married, or Both?*

A man and a woman spend all their days off and holidays together.
Dating, Married, or Both?

A man and a woman are sexually active.
Dating, Married, or Both?

A man and a woman put their money together and buy an iPod.
Dating, Married, or Both?

A man and woman decide which one of them will have the final decision on everything. *Dating, Married, or Both?*

Okay, so how was it? Was it hard to decide on some of them if the couple was just dating or married? Or were they all crystal clear? If you had trouble choosing on a few or all of them, then **B4UD8** you need to learn that dating is not marriage, and for that reason there are tons of things that are different between the two. So let's dig in and see why dating is not marriage.

The Difference between Dating and Marriage

What is dating? That question sounds stupid and obvious at the same time. But go with it. Hopefully you've already decided on the purpose for dating and gotten some basic thoughts on what happens on a date and why. So what is dating? Here are a few things to consider when answering that question:

1. Dating is a means to an end—the end of dating. How many people do you know who all they want to do all their lives is date? They just want to date and date and date for the rest of their lives. Not many? Any? Chances are not many people say all I want to do is find someone to date forever. Because for most people, dating has a purpose. It's a means to an end, and that end is finding the one you wanna marry. Dating isn't the eternal lifestyle for a couple who loves each other. It's just the way to get to the goal: marriage. Okay, so we've said it enough. Dating is just a means to an end.

2. Dating is temporary. If dating is a means to an end, that means it should end. Therefore it is temporary. There's no ring, no signed documents pledging till death do us part. When you date someone there are only two outcomes: you will either break up or get married. In both instances you're gonna stop dating.

3. Dating is an experiment. It's a test to see if this thing is gonna stick. It's a way to explore how well two people get along and how much they want to be together. In more purposeful instances, it might seem less experimental and more a formality. A way to spend the time needed in preparation for marriage. But in either instance, there is still a chance that this combination might not take and the couple will break things off before tying the knot.

4. Dating involves at least two individuals. When you date it's you and another independent person, both of you with your own lives, own feelings, and own bodies. The two people involved in dating live in different houses, sleep in different beds, and have different families. They haven't become one and they haven't involved the hearts of the rest of their extended families. They are two individuals spending time together with a purpose.

I'm not marrying you until you can afford a place big enough for the both of us.

So do any of those ideas about dating shock you? Have you in the past or are you right now dating in a way that doesn't jive with these ideas? Or have you found that in your experience this is exactly what dating is? Maybe you have no experience, and so this all seems well and good. No matter where you've come from, **B4UD8** it's important to know where you are going. And one of the most important things to understand is the difference between dating and marriage. It might seem kinda obvious, but love relationships can be a slippery slope to looking a whole lot like marriage if you're not careful. The lines can get blurred in the heat of the moment, when love is blinding your vision like a gaze into the sun. So **B4UD8**, get into your mind the difference between dating and marriage.

Let's take a look at **marriage** so that you can see the differences right here.

1. Marriage is the end of dating. Once you get married you are no longer dating. You will never date the same way again. You are married, and the goal of your dating life has arrived. Unlike dating, marriage isn't a means to an end, it is the goal and a state of being for the rest of your life. Sure, you might have "date night" with your spouse, but that's to maintain your relationship, not investigate the possibilities or get to know each other.

2. Marriage is permanent. Unlike dating, marriage is a lifetime commitment, till death do you part. F-O-R-E-V-E-R! It is not a means to an end, it is the end. Or as some of us like to think of it, the beginning, the beginning of a new life.

3. Marriage involves a whole family. When two people get married, a new family is started. She takes his name, they become one physically and emotionally, even financially. And the new life begins. They merge both sides of the family to make one extended family. They all care for each other like family does.

Okay, make sense? See how marriage isn't dating and dating isn't marriage? So why a whole chapter on the subject? Well, because as obvious

Michael,

When I was younger, I thought dating was practically marriage, it just wasn't official. After all, that's the purpose of dating, right? Imitate what it would be like to be married to see if you like the person. At least that was my twisted way of thinking. So if I wanted to add something to my social calendar I cleared it with the other person, and I expected that of her. Because I practiced dating as mini-marriage I became a serial monogamist. Trouble is, when we broke up it was mini-divorce. We got hurt and so did the others we brought into our mini-marriage. The breakup took more work than normal breakups because we had to unravel our entwined lives. I hurt so many people by pretending that dating was marriage. It made the relationships harder on everyone involved.

as it seems, many people still confuse the two once they start to date. Instead of looking at dating as it is, a temporary and experimental means to an end between two individuals, they look at it as a permanent conclusion to dating that involves the whole family until the next breakup. And they start playing house. You probably know couples like this, couples who have been dating so long and are so close that they are like an old married couple. It seems cute. They seem so close and everyone is so jealous, but the truth is that they just might have gone too far. They have started to pretend they are married without really being married, and there are all kinds of dangers that pop up when you do that. Let's have a look.

The Dangers of Playing House

When a couple who are only dating start to pretend like they are married, they start to believe they deserve and can have all the perks of marriage. They play house as if they had the commitment, the rings, and the legal document stating till death do us part. But they don't, and so the trouble comes.

Sean and Kara were the perfect couple. He was the star quarterback, she was the perky blonde cheerleader. Everyone loved them and they loved each other. You would never see one without the other. Ask Kara if she could go to a movie tonight with you and your friends, and she'd have to call Sean first to see if it was okay.

Since they were together so much, they spent a lot of time with each other's families. They had dinners together, went on family vacations to-gether, and spent every holiday going from his family's functions to her family's functions. They were the ultimate couple. Everyone envied them but also teased them about being like an old married couple, though everyone knew they would be together forever.

But one day things changed. Sean and Kara broke it off. No one was sure if it was Kara who said good-bye because she had another guy on the side, or if it was Sean who broke it off because he wanted to be free to move out of town and go to the university he'd worked so hard to get into. But no matter what it was, they were done. The old married couple divorced after all those years of dating bliss.

Sean and Kara made the monumental mistake of playing house, pretending like they were a married couple when they were really only a dating couple. And because of that big mistake they did a lot of things they now regret. They went places a dating couple should never go, and they both paid the price emotionally and physically. Even though they've long since moved on, married for real, and started families, they still wish they hadn't done all the stuff they did.

Playing house gets you into all kinds of trouble and makes the heartache of divorce, a.k.a. break-ing up, more painful than it needs to be. There are so many areas in which thinking of dating as marriage can get you into trouble, so many ways that it can make it harder to be faithful and harder to be clean and guilt free. If you want to date with a purpose and take care of your temple then you

I learned my lesson. Last time I played house I tied up traffic for hours.

must understand that dating is not marriage and that when you pretend like it is you're faced with all kinds of barriers to a life of godliness.

Sexual Temptation

It's hard enough to control yourself when you are with someone you really, really like, even love, but imagine loving that person and pretending like you are married. Suddenly, what is in the way of going all the way? Not much. If you are, after all, practically married, then what is to stop you? And so sexual temptation is a huge danger for couples who are playing house. If you are dating someone you know is the one, who you plan to marry, and who you have all but given your name to, or taken the name of, then look out, you run the risk of playing house.

Marriage is an amazing thing, and it comes with its perks. One of the biggest of those is sex. There's no denying it. God created something awesome for husbands and wives to share. Each other. It's the one way we can enjoy another person in that way without any guilt or danger. It's the ultimate for a couple in love. And if a couple isn't married but pretending like they are, then they are lying to themselves and messing up the temple by allowing someone in that isn't authorized by God to be there. You're basically sneaking someone into the temple that doesn't belong there, doing things that aren't allowed until your temple and your future spouse's temple have been made one before God.

5 Stupid Things U Think B4U Play House

- We'll be together forever, so why not go all the way?
- We'll be together forever, so why not live together?
- We'll be together forever, so why not mix finances?
- We'll be together forever, so why not go on vacation together?
- We'll be together forever, so why not buy major purchases together?

B4UD8, you have to agree that dating is not marriage and that you aren't going to allow it to become a pretend marriage; otherwise you run an even bigger risk of sexual sin.

Practicing Divorce

Dating someone for a long time seems like an amazing thing. You celebrate each month anniversary as if to say, "Look, we made it to another one, we are so meant to be!" It's certainly the better option when you consider the other one is to say "Well, we didn't make it another month. We broke up." But there is a danger in long-term relationships; they can start to feel like marriage. Even if you promise that you aren't acting all married, or going all the way, you can still feel very connected. You meld your lives together. You share clothes, money, cars, even toothbrushes. You know everything about each other. You need each other. And it all seems great, but what happens when you break up? Well, probably after you get your heart back into one piece you start to date again. And since you are someone who is good at long-term relationships, you find another one and off you go. And maybe the pattern repeats itself once more, twice more, or more and more until you find the one you wanna marry. So what's happened in that time? Well, you've had a bunch of long-term, very committed relationships that you have ended for one reason or another. And in all that, you've gotten really good at leaving or being left by the one you love. In a word, divorcing. When a couple plays house they risk more than sexual junk, they risk getting really good at divorce. At not putting up with little imperfections that everyone has, including your future "perfect" mate. Practice makes perfect. All that you do when you break up a lot is learn that you can do it, you can live through it, and even how to make it happen. Breaking up is a good way to end a bad relationship, but it's also a good way to learn to say, "If I'm not happy, I'm just gonna move on." And so as dating is the means to an end (marriage), breaking up from multiple deep relationships becomes the training ground for getting really good at divorce. Learning the art of rejection is important, but it has to go hand in hand with not getting too deep, too soon.

B4UD8, realize that dating isn't meant to be permanent. It isn't marriage, and the more you date deeply and break up, the more accepting you get of divorce.

Emotional Manipulation

Another danger of playing house is the use of emotional manipulation. There was once this guy named Ryan who had been dating Jessica for almost three years. And his parents loved her! They took her with them everywhere, and his mom even called her just to chat. They wanted a daughter-in-law, and they wanted it to be Jess. So when Ryan realized he just wasn't in love with Jessica anymore, he had a dilemma. If he broke up with her, he would break not only her heart but his family's heart as well. Could he do that to his mom? How would his sister react to losing her "sister Jess"? Ryan was stuck. He didn't want to marry Jess, but what could he do now? It was too late. And so Ryan did what his family wanted and he asked Jessica to marry him, all the while wishing he could be man enough to just tell everyone he wasn't in love. By the time Ryan found the courage to tell Jess she wasn't the one, the date had been set, the dress bought, and the invitations sent, and it was even more painful a split than anyone could have imagined if it had happened a few months earlier.

When you date someone and make them part of your family, you run the risk of emotional manipulation. Not that your family is manipulating you, necessarily, but you run the risk of lying to yourself. You say things like Ryan said about Jessica. "I don't want to be with her, but if I break up with her my mom will die." And suddenly your life isn't yours anymore. Or maybe you'll have the strength to go ahead and break it up. But then you have to spend months, years, picking up the

Michael,

I remember a streak where either the family loved me and the girl was "meh," or the girl was falling hard and her fam hated me. It was bananas.

Hayley,

I guess I broke that streak. After one trail ride at my dad's horse ranch, he came back hooked.

Michael,

I think he was just happy you weren't going to be an old crazy cat lady!

pieces of your and your family's broken hearts. If dating isn't marriage, then that means your girlfriend or boyfriend doesn't become part of the family. They don't get the perks of marriage without all the legalities and commitments. Don't enjoy the temporary high of playing house at the expense of your future happiness and the mental and emotional health of your family.

Losing Your Emotional Virginity

Another danger of long-term relationships that look and feel like a mini-marriage is the risk to your emotional virginity. A natural outcome of dating, especially for a long time, is emotional intimacy. That means the longer you date and the closer you feel, the more you share your heart and your feelings. And as you do, you start to go places emotionally that you shouldn't go unless you are married. In the physical realm it's easy to understand the concept of losing your virginity, but when it comes to your emotions it's a lot more difficult to spot. But the same kind of bonding that happens from sexual intimacy can happen emotionally as well. Two people can start to feel connected because of all they've shared of themselves. They start to say things like, "No one knows me as well as you do" and "We've been through so much together; I could never leave you." And bonds are made, very strong ones. That might sound wonderful, but since dating isn't permanent, dating relationships were never meant to go so deep. The emotional oneness is meant for marriage, and playing around with it while acting married just weakens the power of marriage.

There are a lot of ways you can lose your emotional virginity and lots of things you can do that can be a slippery slope to losing it, just as fooling around physically is a slippery slope. If you are practicing any of these things in a relationship, then you've just started down the slippery slope to losing your emotional virginity. So beware.

Sharing your most darkest secrets with each other. Part of getting to know someone is sharing with them, it's true, but just watch it, because the more you share, the more you bond, and the more you bond, the more painful it is when you separate. The only permanent relationship according to God's Word is marriage. And there are many reasons for that, but one of them is because the two become one and breaking apart one is very painful for everyone involved. God knows that the closer you get to someone, the more you will be hurt by separation. If you aren't married to the person, then don't bond yourself to them too tightly. As you share your darkest secrets with them, a funny thing happens—it's like they become a part of you. They get you. They start to know you more than anyone, and your emotional virginity is lost. You're attached much more than you were meant to be. So be careful about sharing too much before you become engaged. Sure, you need to know each other and be open, but bonding prematurely can lead to disaster.

Relying on the one you are dating to be your hope, your way out of a bad life. If your life is miserable and you want a change, it can be very tempting to play house with the one you love in order to pretend like they are your salvation, your way out of a bad situation. But you can't let a person other than Jesus become your salvation. When you do, you put too much pressure on them, and it eventually destroys the relationship. That role was meant for Jesus and Jesus alone. So never rely on the person you are dating to save you.

Getting so close that you would die if you ever lost them. Being so close to someone that you can't live without them is a real goal of dating for most people. The trouble is that it's not always a mutual thing. It's great to fall in love and to desire to be with someone forever, but never, ever even utter the words "I would die without you," because that means that person has become your idol, the thing for which you live. And as a believer, you should not be living for anyone but your God. When people start to pretend to be married while they are just dating, they start to think they can't live without each other, and when and if that breakup comes, some horrible pain can result. And if that pain is accompanied by a heart that believes it will die without the other person, that heart is often prone to think of ending the pain permanently by doing just what it promised, dying without the other person. It's dangerous to say you would die without anyone but especially dangerous when you say that or think that about someone you are dating.

Praying together and/or doing Bible study together. How can prayer and Bible study

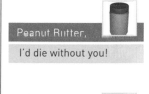
Peanut Butter,
I'd die without you!

Jelly,
Naw, eventually you'd just find yourself totally into another cookie.

be wrong? It sounds ridiculous, doesn't it? But the truth is that when you pray together you create emotional bonds with one another. And sometimes they are real but other times they are imagined. Prayer can even be a kind of aphrodisiac that excites you and makes the other person more attractive. But what you are really attracted to is Christ in them. And though you should be attracted to the spiritual side of the person you date, you have to be careful not to let that attraction lead to sexual tension and eventually sexual intimacy. The closer you feel to someone, the easier it is to fool around with them. So you have to be careful with such powerful and emotional things like prayer and studying God's Word. They are things you should be doing but not with the person you are dating, unless you have a ring and a wedding date. As preparation for marriage it starts to make sense, but until then you just may be playing with fire.

Asking permission from each other. Sometimes couples who play house can create emotional chains around each other by demanding that their significant other ask permission before doing things without them. The thing that those couples forget is that dating is not marriage, and therefore there is never a need to ask permission from your bf or gf unless you're breaking or rearranging plans. Sure, you can see how they would feel about you doing this or that, but they can never restrict you from doing something like a spouse could. If you are asking permission to do anything without your "other," then you've lost your emotional virginity and you've created a big mess for yourself. The trouble with the whole permission thing is that it gives too much honor to a relationship that is not meant to be honored like marriage. Since dating is not marriage, it shouldn't be treated with the same reverence. Asking permission gives the impression that you are owned by the other person, or managed by them. A kid asks permission from their parents, whose God-given and legal job it is to take care of them and feed and shelter them. An adult asks permission of their boss to take a vacation because the boss pays them to come to work. But a girlfriend does not ask permission from her boyfriend to go out Friday night with her best friend. Asking permission implies they are responsible for you or you are responsible for them, and that's not the case when you are dating. When you date, never ask permission from your significant other as if they own you or possess authority over you.

How to Date without Pretending You're Married

- Don't submit to one another like a married couple.
- No shacking up.
- Don't mix your finances.
- No spending family vacations and holidays together.
- No staying the night.
- No sexual intimacy.
- No calling the other's parents "Mom" and "Dad"

B4Ugo

Okay, so hopefully we've made our case. Dating is not marriage, and it's hard enough to keep from messing up without playing house. When you pretend that dating is marriage you make all kinds of mistakes. **B4UD8**, you've got to make a promise to yourself and God that you won't steal all the perks of marriage while you are only dating. God made marriage for a specific purpose, and unless you are married you are not to pretend like you are. God says that when a couple gets married they become one flesh. And becoming one flesh with someone you aren't married to is fornication. If you've ever been to church, then you probably heard that fornication is a sin. Becoming one with someone without the covenant of marriage is a sin. **B4UD8**, you've got to decide if you want to take God at his Word and refuse to make up your own rules. If that is the case then understand that dating is not marriage and you are not responsible to your crush like you would be to a spouse.

> So they are no longer two but one. Therefore, don't let anyone separate what God has joined together.
>
> Matthew 19:6

Working Through It

Okay, now's your chance to let this stuff simmer. Think about your thoughts on dating, your past experiences, and your future dreams.

How does it feel to hear that dating is temporary?

In what ways do you feel you have already lost your emotional virginity? How can you protect those areas going forward?

What are three differences between dating and marriage that you agree with?

Are there any differences between dating and marriage that you don't agree with?

Why do you think people feel compelled to share their deepest secrets with the one they are dating?

How much information is TMI?

Take this quiz to see what you are thinking:

I think that I should tell my date every-thing there is to know about me.
True   False

I believe in true love at first sight.
True   False

I think that praying together is a healthy way to bond. *True   False*

I want my bf/gf to always ask my permis-sion before they make plans. *True   False*

I think it's okay to move in together if you are engaged. *True   False*

My life is nothing without someone else.
True   False

Okay, so how'd you do? The answer is yours to decide. You can make up your own mind when it comes to your life. But if you've answered

B4UD8 DEFINITION

NQEITBAJO *[en-quit-ba-ho]*
Not quite enough information to base a judgment on

mostly true then it looks like you think dating and marriage are the same thing except for the legalities. And if that's you, then just beware—you are walking a dangerous line, one that it's very easy to slip off of into sexual sin. When you equate dating with marriage, you equate everything that goes along with marriage as okay for you. Get the picture?

If you answered mostly false to these Qs then you seem to have a good understanding of the differences between and dangers of thinking of your bf/gf like a spouse.

Take some time to talk over the differences between dating and marriage with someone you know and trust who is already married. Think about how you view dating and the amount of honor you put upon it along with how much freedom you think it gives you with each other.

HAYLEY & MICHAEL **DiMARCO**

7 THINGS YOU NEED TO KNOW BEFORE YOUR NEXT DATE

B4UD8

For everything
we couldn't squeeze into the book,
log on to B4UD8.com!

Q4U | *from B4UD8.com*

My boyfriend and I have been dating for five years. We are very close and do everything together. For Christmas we are always with each other and so we take turns going to each other's family's. This year his family is taking a trip to Hawaii and it's his turn to be with my family. He really wants to go to Hawaii but he doesn't want to hurt me since it's our family's year. I think he may go anyway, but I want him to stay with me. Maybe I could go with him, but it's not my turn to go with his family. I don't know what to do, it's so hard having two families to please. Help!

Maya

Dear Maya,

This sounds familiar. In fact, husbands and wives the world over struggle with this same problem every year. But they're in a slightly different position than you because they are *married*. Sounds like you and your boyfriend are a bit confused. See, dating is not marriage, and that means you don't share family functions like married people. You each have your own family and should enjoy your own family things alone until, if ever, you are married to each other. When you arrange your dating life like a married life you get way too close way too fast. Marriage is meant to be forever, dating is not. Dating relationships end in either a break up or a wedding; either way, dating is temporary.

That said, it sounds like it's time for you two to go your separate ways this Christmas. Let him be with his family while you stay with yours. It isn't fair to either group to make them have to lose time with their kids on this important holiday. It can be hard to make the transition from playing house to acting more like you are two different people with two different families, but in the end it will only make your relationship healthier and your families happier.

We know u have the Q's. We have the A's! Log on to B4UD8.com to make the exchange.

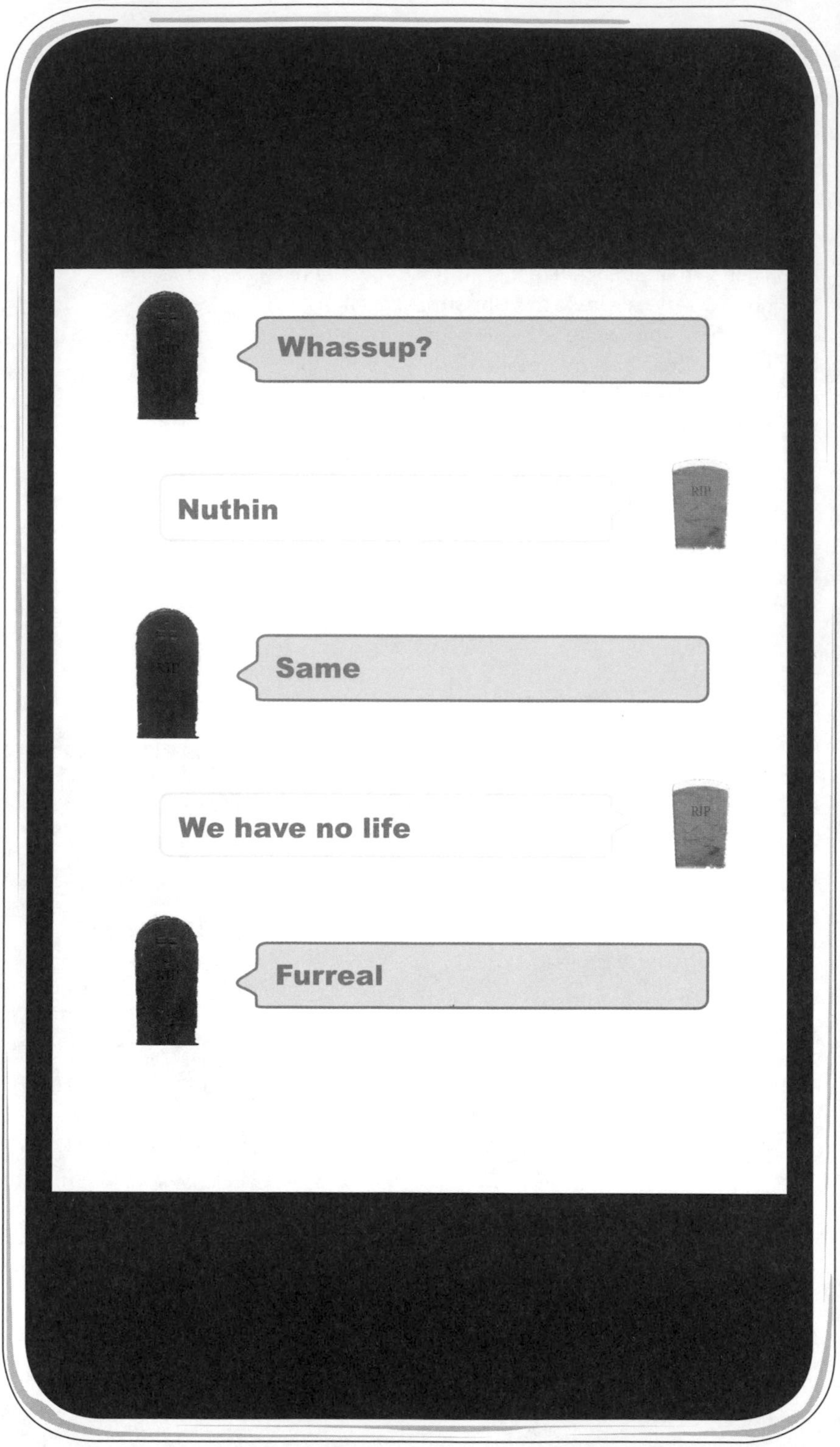
Whassup?
Nuthin
Same
We have no life
Furreal

4: Have a Life

The fourth thing you need to know **B4UD8** is you have to have a life. Having a life has to do with being an individual. Remember, you aren't married. You aren't one with another person yet. So you each have your own lives. Lots of couples make a fatal error when they give up everyone and everything that makes them who they are in order to be with each other. It feels really good at first and seems almost irresistible, but when you give up your life, you're gonna have to work hard to try to get it back when things get rough, you break up, or you just get bored with each other. There is no way that another person can be or should be your everything. There is only one being who can fill that tall order, and his name is God. When you make the other person your entertainment, your pastime, your joy, your hope, your everything, you slowly kill the very thing you were hoping to give life to. So **B4UD8**, learn how to have a life.

Dating Disasters

For Misha and Jake it was love at first sight. They both said they went to bed thinking of each other and woke up thinking of each other. It was dating ecstasy, the kind that's like food to the soul. The kind that makes you forget to eat and even forget to sleep. The almost heavenly kind that's oh-so-hard to resist. So at first they called each other every night and talked for hours. Then they started to spend every Friday and Saturday connected at the hip. Pretty soon, they got so they just couldn't bear to be apart, so they spent every spare moment together. Friends would ask them to do this or that, and they would consider it, but given the choice between doing something with a friend and doing something with the love of their lives, they always chose love. And pretty soon the invitations stopped, and they were glad. No more saying no to friends. And more time for each other. But after a year of dating bliss, things started to change. Jake got restless. A new girl in his class caught his eye. He realized he was getting tired of Misha. She was smothering him, never doing anything without him, always calling to find out where he was. It was too much. So he dropped the ax and broke up with her. Misha felt like she would explode. She didn't understand it. And to make matters worse, she had to see Jake with his new girl every day at lunch. It was sheer torture. She needed someone to talk to, but who was there? All her friends were nowhere to be found. She had ditched them so many times that they wrote her off. They moved on, and Misha was left with no one to cry to but her cat.

When Alexa started dating Trent he was pure perfection to her. He was star of the basketball team. He was super popular and super cute. And Alexa loved it. She loved all the things they did with their friends. She loved going out in big groups and being the center of attention. She loved the laughter and the jokes. She just loved life. But over time it seemed like there were fewer and fewer friends to hang out with. They did so much together that Trent started to skip out of social functions with his friends, and the gang slowly broke up. Now, even though Alexa still thought Trent was cute and awesome, she felt like something was missing. What happened to the popular, busy guy she fell in love with? What happened to the parties and the trips to the lake with the gang? Alexa still had lots of friends, but Trent seemed to be too needy. He came with her when she went out with the girls, he called her every night even when she was staying the night at a friend's. He was so clingy. "Can't you just go hang out with your friends? I'm tired of being the only person you hang out with. What happened to you? You used to have a life, now you need to get one!" And that was the end of that. Alexa moved on, and Trent was left chasing after a girl who had just grown tired of him.

In both of these relationships the couples overdid it. Have you ever heard the expression "too much of a good thing"? It's true. No matter how hyped you are to be with someone, you've got to give it a break. Too much time together will do two things. It will burn you out on each other and it will burn your friendship bridges behind you. So **B4UD8** it's important to have a life and then to learn to keep that life alive and kickin'.

The Dangers of Losing a Life

B4UD8 you have a life. You have friends, hobbies, things you do with your family. A life.

Hayley,

I can totally relate to this. I have dated some guys who were way overboard. At first I liked the attention, but after a couple of weeks it was just too much. Too much responsibility to be the source of all their happiness. It made me uncomfortable and made me want to get away. I like romance and attention as much as the next girl, but when it's nonstop it loses its luster. The guy who was able to hold back and not smother me but give me attention and then give me space too, was the one I ultimately married. Nice work, honey!

Michael,

Thanks, babe. Yeah, I knew that you like romance but also that you can have too much of a good thing. When you got to anticipate it, you were much happier than if it was the steady diet. But I have to say, this lesson I was slow to learn. For the longest time I thought the answer to romance was quality AND quantity. Glad I tamed the tiger before I met you (B4IMETU).

Maybe not the perfect life, but at least you are living, doing, being. But once you start to date, a silly thing can happen. You take that life, that day-to-day, busy-doing-things life and you lose it. You don't do it on purpose, and you don't do it all of a sudden, but you do it. And then you are left without a life of your own, just the life of "us," as you call it. We do this, we do that. Did they invite us? Is that for us? And me becomes we. That might sound like the perfect life, and for a married couple it is, but when people who are dating lose their individual lives, they risk a lot of things emotionally, spiritually, and physically. And here are some of those things.

Sexual Temptation

Sex is always a temptation when you are dating someone. It's always lurking in the back of your minds. And that's normal, because if the purpose of dating is to find the one you want to marry, then sex could one day be a permissible and pleasurable activity in that relationship. But when you are dating, you want to do all you can to avoid messing up sexually. For the obvious reasons like STDs and pregnancy, but also for the spiritual reasons like sin and uh, oh yeah, sin. So let's agree that sexually tempting situations aren't the best thing for you. Now, if your bf/gf is your life, the sexual temptation stuff gets even more intense. The reason is that you will find yourselves alone a lot, and that's just asking for trouble. But another reason is that you lose your support system. Your peeps who help keep you accountable are no longer in the picture, or at least are way in the background, and you don't have anyone who has your back spiritually. Sexual temptation is hard enough to handle with the help of your trusted circle, but handling it alone is even harder. So in order to save yourself from risking disobedience to God, you've got to keep your life going. Keep your friends. Do things with them. Don't spend every spare moment with your gf/bf, and your risk for messing up sexually can go way down.

Becoming Self-Obsessed

As believers we are called to be selfless, thinking more highly of others than of ourselves. The trouble with ditching all your friends and spending all your time with the one you love is that it's all about you. I know, it sounds like it's all about them, but it's not. It's all about you and making you feel good. Making you feel fulfilled. Making you happy. When left with the choice—do I go out with my friend who really wants to see me tonight or my bf/gf who I really want to see tonight—picking the bf/gf is the self-obsessed choice. It says, "It's all about me and my need for love." And it's pretty ungodly. You have to be careful about giving up caring for others because you are so hot to care about yourself and your honey. It's always best to deny yourself and look to care for others when left with the choice. Besides, if your current crush doesn't appreciate someone that has balance in their life and wants to serve others, they're probably the wrong person for you. So **B4UD8** decide if you want to major on self or on others. Remember, in the end, choosing to go with others will only make your life better than ever. Don't give up the long term in order to be happy in the present.

Hurting Friends and Family

The obvious outcome of choosing yourself and your hormones over friends and family is that ultimately you end up hurting the ones you used to say you loved. When it's always me this and my boyfriend that, it hurts your friends and family. What it says to them is that they are only important as long as you need them, and you don't need them right now, so sayonara! **B4UD8**, make a commitment to yourself never to give up loving your friends and family so you can find a love of your own. You can have both, it just takes balance. Don't sacrifice the ones you love for your own love high.

Suffocating the Relationship

We've talked a lot about how you can hurt the people around you when you ditch them for your new love. But the other thing you ultimately hurt is the relationship. No relationship can live without air. People need room to breathe. And though it might be really great to be with each other nonstop for a season, after a few seasons it can become suffocating. One of the funnest things about dating is the chase. It's exciting not knowing if you're gonna catch that other person or not. It's part of the attraction. Besides, if you're both not ready to get married, then you're not ready to get

Hayley,

It's so weird, but though I don't like to be smothered, I can also get totally obsessed with being in love. I remember when I dated this one guy, he became my best friend. I loved being with him—he was funny, and smart, a good dancer. He liked to do all the things I liked to do, and so we did them all together. Pretty soon, though, I realized that he was my only friend. I liked being with him so much more than my girlfriends that I quit hanging out with them. Bad move. It put too much strain on our relationship, and eventually we broke up. When we did, it was terrible because I didn't have anybody's shoulder to cry on.

Michael,

Hey, I'm a good dancer! Does anyone still do the robot?

caught! But when you give yourself 100 percent to the relationship, the thrill of the chase is gone. If you want to keep the love alive then you have to back off a bit. Be busy sometimes. Do things without your "other" once in a while. Wonder what they are doing. Miss them. And most of all, let them miss you. When you do, the relationship will only get stronger. When you suffocate it by your continual presence, you just weaken it, and one day it will most surely die.

Ignoring Problems

Another danger of losing your life is that it makes it a lot easier to ignore the problems in your relationship. Have you ever heard anyone say, "You're just too close to the problem to see it"? Sometimes when you are so involved in something, like a relationship, and little else, you can get a little blinded. You can't see all the red flags and danger signs that other people outside the relationship can clearly see. If you want another set of eyes, you've got to keep friends and family around. That way, they can tell you if you're a better person because of the relationship or whether you're losing touch with what's important. When you isolate yourself you get into all kinds of trouble. You might not see something your bf/gf is doing to you that is harmful or you might not see what both of you are doing that is killing the relationship. So **B4UD8** make sure that you agree to let your friends and family be a part of your relationship to help you keep on track. -

Michael,

So I'll fall on the grenade on this one. Almost every deep relationship that I got in to way too fast when we really weren't a good match was also during a time in my life when I was isolated from friends and family, and especially isolated in my relationship with God and a local church. Ever buy some shoes or a shirt at the mall that you're all excited about, just to take it home and find it doesn't match anything in your closet? If your closet is full of blues and grays, that orange pair of kicks isn't going to last long. When you ignore red flags in the other person (or yourself), the longer you hang on, the more difficult the return policy. And shoes don't get their feelings hurt.

Forsaking God

The biggest danger you face when you lose your life in order to be with the one you love is you run the risk of forsaking God. It's super easy for your new love to become your best love, even above God. And we don't have to tell you that that's a bad, bad idea. Spending all your time with one person is a bit like worship. You start to give that person the credit for everything you feel and everything you are. When you lose your life, you can easily lose your relationship not only with family and friends but also with God. You stop going to church, you stop doing a Bible study. You don't have time to study or pray, and suddenly you have forsaken your first love and the provider of true love in your life. **B4UD8**, make a plan on how you will keep God number one in your life and never, ever allow a person to take that position. Not for all the short-term happiness in the world.

God's #1! Wildcats #2!

Lots of people think that in order to have a relationship you have to give up everything else. But that's a lie. People who give it all up for love end up broken and lonely when the hard times come. And the hard times will come. You can be sure of that. In this world you will have trouble, it's only natural. But luckily there is a way to soften the impact of that trouble. There is a way that's less difficult, and that is keeping your life. And giving God the number one place in that life. Never let the creation surpass the creator. **B4UD8**, take a look at your life. Is it strong? Could it be stronger? Are you willing to let it go for temporary love?

Or will you hold on to your life so that one day you can gain a love that never ends?

How to Have a Life

Okay, so have you decided? Is having a life the thing for you? If so, then let's dig in to how to do that. How can you take care of your life enough so that it won't ever be lost in the pursuit of love? Let's take a look at the Do's and Don'ts of keeping your life so you can keep a good love alive.

The Don'ts

Don't call every day. This one might seem crazy, especially when you are head over heels. What's the big deal? So you talk on the phone every day. You're getting to know the other person in a safe way. Well, the problem is that when you talk on the phone every day you lose time, time that you could be spending with family, friends, hobbies, and other "your life" stuff. There is no couple on earth that has so much to say that they need to talk on the phone every day. It's not a necessity, it's a pleasure. And too much of a good thing is gluttony. Taking more than you need. You don't need to be on the phone every waking minute. So cut back. Find a way to only talk two or three nights a week. Make a deal with your parents or roommate not to talk every day. It shows restraint, maturity and love for the others who love you. Talking on the phone every night creates an obsession and an obligation. And an obsession is an idol. You should

Tricks for Keeping the Calling Down

Set a hang-up timer. Decide how long you want to talk and time it. When the timer goes off, say "I've gotta run. But I loved talking to you. I'll see you tomorrow." That gets you off the phone and leaves them wanting more. That just helps to keep the love alive. So don't be afraid to hang up.

Make plans. If you usually talk at a certain time, or you have a down spot in your schedule so you know you're gonna want to talk, then make plans. Find things to do to keep you busy. Remember, you want to keep your life for your sake, your friends' sake, and your relationship's sake. Start a night class, make plans with your mom, join a club, do what you can to stay busy so that you can keep a life and get off the phone.

Don't get mad. Now hopefully your bf/gf will see things the same way as you, and if not, then get them their own copy of this book. And don't get mad at them for not calling. Remember the goal and promise to be reasonable. Even if you really, really want to talk every day, don't feel bad that they are sticking to the plan and only calling twice a week. Try to use your noggin and don't get all emotional over something that is really meant to ultimately make your life better.

have no other idols in your life than your God. When you do, everything falls apart. No matter how much fun it is, do yourself and your loved ones a favor and stop talking so much. Create the illusion of a chase. Give each other something to wonder about, something to look forward to. Get busy, keep your life, and you won't run the risk of suffocating a perfectly good relationship.

Don't say no to an invitation from a friend when you have no plans with your "other." Been there, done that. Someone calls and asks you out, but you really are just waiting for the phone to ring so that you and your crush can go hang out, so you say "I'm busy" even though you aren't. Yuck. What a thing to do. If you want to keep your life, then don't say no to an invitation from a friend when you have no plans with your bf/gf. It's hard to think of making plans and then having to say no to your crush when they ask you a few hours later, but that's the way it goes. You have to remember that that just makes you more valuable in their eyes. Because after all, things and people who are in demand are worth much more than things or people no one wants. And sometimes that's the only way you can get time with your friends—by saying no to your crush. It has to be done in order to keep your life. If you say no every time someone else asks you to do something, you're gonna find out that sooner or later they'll stop asking and you'll be all alone. So **B4UD8** make a deal with yourself to not turn down plans with someone other than the one you really want to be with.

Don't ask permission from each other. We've gone over this before, but it bears repeating. Don't ever ask permission from your bf/gf to do something or other unless you already had set plans. You have officially lost your life when you do that. They do not own you. They aren't responsible for you and they aren't your boss, so there is no reason to get their permission. When you start to do that, what you do is give up your right to choose. You give up the responsibility that you have to run your own life, and you give it to someone else. When you do that, it makes you look weak and sold out, sold out to another human being, like a slave. You, as a believer, should not be a slave to anything or anyone other than your God. When you do, you betray him. So never ever ask for permission from the one you are dating; if they are bad they will take advantage of you, and if they are good they will lose interest in a person who has no mind or life of their own. **B4UD8**, learn to make decisions for yourself and never let another person who isn't responsible for you control you.

Don't move in together. Living with someone you aren't married to isn't romantic. It isn't sweet, it isn't even cute, it's just shacking up. Plain and simple. It's cheating the system. Living together is reserved for married people. When you move in with your bf/gf you turn your back on God's law and spit in his face. Living together is nothing but commitment to failure. It says, "We aren't sure of each other enough to make a vow of permanence, so we are going to pretend like we have so we can get all the benefit of marriage without the commitment." It's a bad, bad choice for anyone but especially bad for a believer.

Don't always invite your bf/gf along when you go out with friends or family. You get invited to go out with a group of friends or on a family thing and you say, "Can I bring _____?" "Sure," they say. And why wouldn't they? You go everywhere together. But giving that a break will help you keep your life. There is no reason that your bf/gf has to go with you wherever you go. When you invite them to come along, you tell your friends that they aren't enough, you need her/him to come along to make it worthwhile. It's oftentimes rude, and it makes you look like you aren't an independent person.

> Statistics say that **85 percent** of people who live together before they get married will end up divorced.
>
> Marriagebuilders.com

If they don't invite both of you, then don't ask them. Give them the respect and love they deserve. They might not really care if you do invite your bf/gf, but they will respect you when they see that you don't have to be joined at the hip. So keep your life and give the relationship some breathing room. Do things with friends, alone, when they ask and don't feel guilty for leaving your other dating half out of the equation. If they are a grounded person they will understand and even want you to have a life. - - - - - - - - - - - - -

The Do's

The do list won't take as long, since it's just the opposite of the don't list. But it will be a good review, huh?

Do things with your family alone. You might be tempted to invite your love along on all your family outings, dinners, parties, etc. But don't. Give your family the gift of your presence. Be with them. Talk with them and keep the love alive so that you can keep your life.

Do make plans with friends without your crush. Make plans. Promise to do things, even on the weekends, without your crush tagging along. Not all the time, but at least a couple times a week do things with your friends one on one so they can get your full and undivided attention and know that you haven't left them for the pursuit of love.

Do keep doing the things you love. If you have hobbies, sports, things in your life that you

Michael,

You know why people shack up? Because it feels good. Financially, socially, and yup, sexually. It totally has benefits, or so we tell ourselves. The benefits are obvious, but what people tend to ignore is those benefits are only beneficial when two people have a social and spiritual contract to stay together forever. Let's call this revolutionary contract "marriage." Before I got serious about my faith, I was a shacker. All that's good about it and why people like it is because it's all the frosting of marriage without the cake—the honor and commitment.

loved to do before you started dating, don't stop doing them for love. Keep them up. Sure, you might cut back on some of them so you can add time with them, but don't give it up completely. In fact, if you don't have a favorite pastime, then it's time to get one. Find something that can keep you busy and keep you from having to be with your crush all the time. You've got to start to make a life for yourself so that you can have something to offer and something to do when and if this relationship ever ends.

Do keep going to church. A lot of times it's hard to stay active at church once a true love (or something like it) comes along. Lots of people just go to church to find someone to date, and that makes it even harder to keep going. But the truth is that no love is as lasting as the love of God. And you must continue to nurture and respect that relationship even after you have a new love in your life. So keep going to church. Do church activities; stay busy so that you can keep your life.

B4Ugo

If you don't have a life, you need to getchu one. Having a life makes living more doable and more fun. Just as much as you need a life in order to find the one, you have to keep that life after you find them. People are attracted to other people who are busy, active, happy, and loved. Don't become a hermit as soon as you find love; it only makes you less attractive and less loved by those who used to be a part of your life. **B4UD8** it's very important to learn the value of doing things with your friends and family. Build relationships that will last so that they can laugh with you, love with you, and cry with you. Friends and family are an extension of God's hand. They are one way that he hugs you and talks to you. They can share truth with you and keep you on track. Don't let the pursuit of human love interfere with what God has planned for you. The life you could be giving up to be with your new love might just be the life God had planned for you to live. Don't walk away from where you are to get to what you think you want without making sure that God is in the middle of it all. Keeping your life with all your friends, family, and church will help you to keep God at the center of it all and make you a much more desirable person for the one you want anyway.

Working Through It

Do you think you can date and have a life at the same time?

What ways have you messed up and lost your life in dating relationships?

What are some things you'd like to do in the future in order to have a life?

Why do you think it's so hard to keep from putting all your strength into your date?

If you are dating, how many minutes/hours a day do you talk on the phone with your bf/gf?

What scares you about not seeing each other so much?

Q4U | *from B4UD8.com*

I Need Some Guy Time

My girlfriend has a problem with me doing things with my guy friends without her. She says I am selfish when I hang out with them because she wants to be with me. I love being with her, but sometimes I just want to be alone with the guys. Nothing against her, it's just a guy thing. How do I get her to understand that it isn't about her and that I really need some time off?

Jake

Dear Jake,

It can be hard for a girl to understand why her boyfriend doesn't want to be with her 24/7, especially if that's what she wants. When someone is in love they want to be with the person all the time and can easily get jealous of times when they are away, especially when they are having fun. But that doesn't mean you can't spend time away from her, it just means she's going to have to learn how to survive without you and how to have a life of her own. You might think you are caring for her by giving in and not going out with the guys, but what you are really doing is enabling her to be weak and helpless. If she is to become a strong and confident woman she has to learn to spend time without you. She can't make you her everything but has to find a way to have other friends and interests. If she doesn't, she will eventually end up smothering you and driving you away with her neediness. So help her understand that time away is good for you both and it only makes you like her and want her more. Let her know that you need her to let you do this in order to keep the relationship alive and healthy. Don't let her convince you of anything different but be empathetic and understanding of her "needs." When you eventually marry, her or anyone else, this exercise will help you to become a strong leader and a caring husband. Smart men and women know how to help those they love to maintain healthy lives, even if healthy isn't something they are particularly interested in.

OK, so you know about the Q's, but have you checked out the online confessional? Anonymously dump your trip-ups at B4UD8.com.

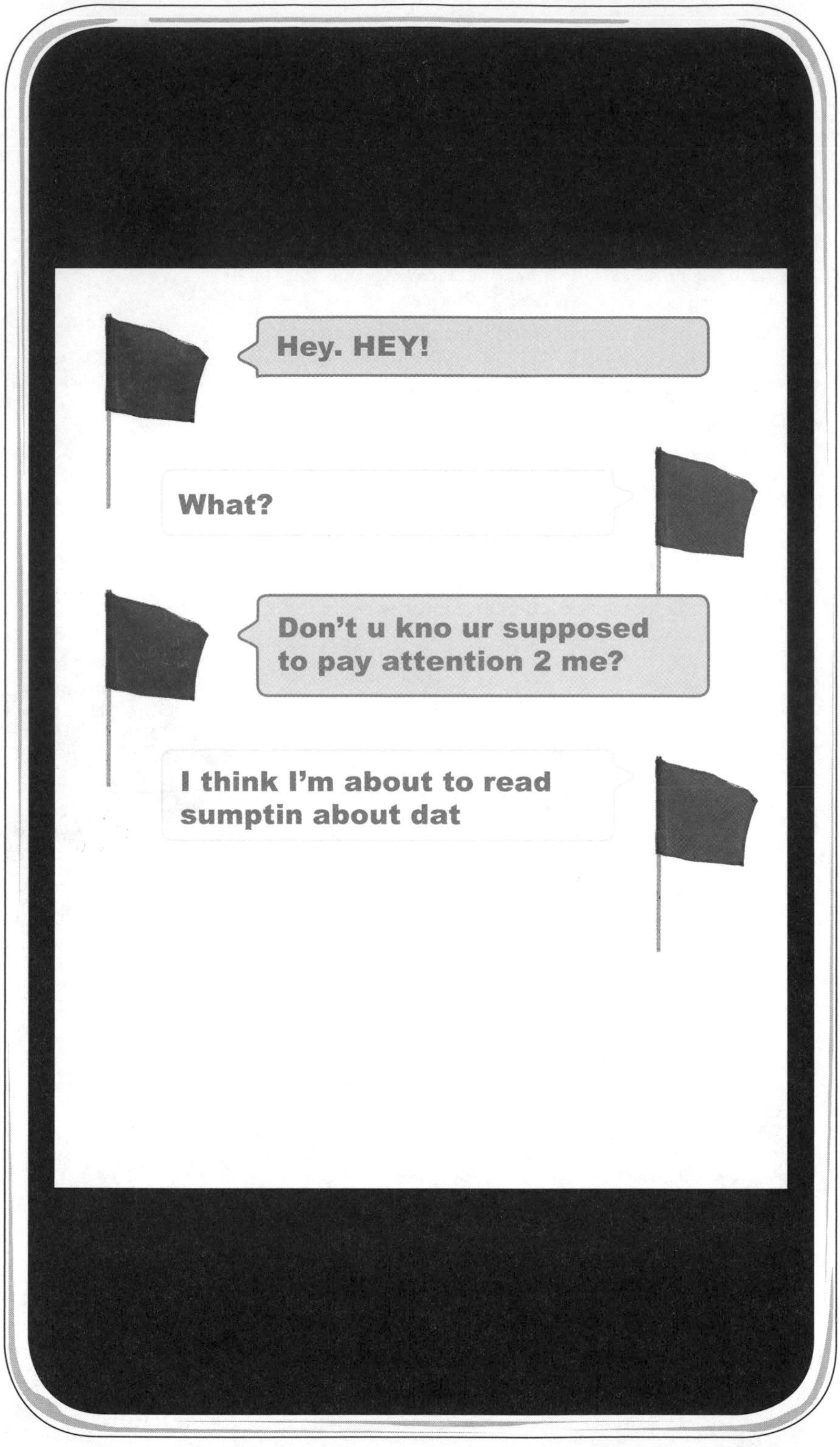
Hey. HEY!
What?
Don't u kno ur supposed to pay attention 2 me?
I think I'm about to read sumptin about dat

5: Red Flags Are Red for a Reason

The fifth thing you should know **B4UD8** is that red flags are red for a reason. Red flags are warnings. Small things that you see, hear, or feel that tell you something might be wrong. Just like with stoplights, these red flags should get you to stop and look around before you go any further. If you don't stop when you see a red flag you run the risk of driving right off the road or smashing into oncoming traffic. You have to be willing to look at the red flags flying in front of you if you want to ultimately choose a good dating relationship.

Red flags aren't always constant. They might show themselves for a split second and then they are gone. Or they might be hanging out for everyone to see. When someone wears their red flag proudly, it can be kinda hard to even think of it as red. They might claim, "Oh no, this isn't a danger sign, it's just a cool color that I like to wear in order to stand out. It makes me unique!" But since red flags are really red for a reason, **B4UD8** you have to be willing to watch the signals and not shut your eyes, cover your ears, and yell "umna, umna, umna" until the red flags go away. If you aren't willing to look at the red flags in your relationship then all bets are off. And the heartache is on.

So why don't we take a look at some red flags and see how you would handle them if you should see them hanging over your current crush.

What Is a Red Flag in a Dating Relationship?

If you've decided that dating is the time to figure out if you like a person enough to be with them the rest of your life, then finding the red flags now, while you've got the chance, is a really good idea. Even if you aren't dating in order to find your future "forever," it's still a good idea to watch for red flags before they take you down a dangerous or heartbreaking road. When you date, no matter what your goal is, it's a time when you are both watching each other to see if there is anything you really, really like or really, really hate that would make or break the relationship. And because of that most of the time people are on their best behavior at least in the beginning of a dating relationship. We all feel kind of like salesmen wanting to close the deal or an applicant applying for a job. "Do you want me? See how great I am?" We want to be liked, we want to be loved, and we definitely don't want to be judged. And that's what makes it hard to see what color flags might be flying. So in order to see the red flags in your date, you're gonna have to switch out of the "you're perfect and everything you say and do is perfect" mode and be a little bit more discerning. That means you're gonna have to ask some questions, listen to the answers, and then see if there is anything in you that spots a red flag. You might just get an inkling or a little thought in your head that says "Wait a minute. That seems kinda weird. What did I just hear?" Or you might not see anything red about them, but your friend might see a big ol' flag as clear as day and point it out to you. There might even be people who aren't your friends helping you to spot red flags. That usually happens from hearing rumors or warnings from people who know the one you're crushing on. No matter how you are introduced to a red flag, it's important to take them seriously. Don't project perfection onto an imperfect person.

Lots and lots of people see red flags in relationships and just look the other way. Somehow love (or the pursuit of love) overpowers the red flags and blocks them from view. And that can work for a while, but eventually the thing the red flag was signaling will pop up and refuse to be ignored. At that point you'll be looking at some major drama in your life courtesy of Red Flags 'R' Us, not to mention a whole lot of cleaning up to do.

So now let's take a look at some common red flags that you might not be looking at right now but will be good prep for you to think about **B4UD8**.

Some Dangerous Red Flags

Red flags signal danger and shouldn't be ignored. Some things that look like red flags might not be red flags after all, but you can't make assumptions. When you see a red flag, you need to check it out and make sure it's truly red. So here are some popular flags that lots of dating people refuse to look into.

If you see any of this stuff in someone you are dating, pull the car over and get out. Don't get caught up in the fun or "potential" of the relationship. Keep watch and stop things before they get out of hand.

Abusive or Controlling

This one seems so obvious to everyone but the person in the middle of it. It's a weird thing, but when you are being abused it's really hard to acknowledge it to yourself. Something psychological takes the love you feel (or want to feel) for the person as proof positive that they would never abuse you and so you must be crazy or something. If you are dating someone who is abusive or controlling then that's a huge red flag. This is the kind of red flag that signals that there is nothing but a big cliff and a big fall in front of you. So stop and don't go any further. If you do, you'll be in for a world of hurt. Remember that stuff about taking care of the temple? Well, this is when that comes in handy. If you are no longer your own but Christ's, then you've got to protect his temple. You can't allow anyone you date, no matter how much you love them, to abuse you or control you.

You Feel Worse after Spending Time with Them

If you feel worse after spending time with your bf/gf then you've got a big red flag waving in front of your face. It's not normal or healthy to feel worse after being with someone. The things they say or do might be subtle, you might not notice it on the surface, but deep down you just feel worse. When all their anger beats you down, wears you out, and makes you doubt yourself, you are in a bad relationship. It's not a good feeling, but it's a good clue that you are looking at a red flag. So if you are dating someone and they make you feel bad about yourself, then stop it. Stop the relationship and refuse to pollute or destroy God's temple.

Sexually Pushy

Another red flag that you can't afford to miss is if they are sexually pushy. If someone is pushing you to do more than you know you should, or more than you want to do, then they are being pushy. It's not cute or sexy that they want you so much. It doesn't prove how much they love you. And giving in to their pushiness doesn't prove to them that you love them. It just proves that they've overpowered you, and therefore you are weak and controllable. Yuck! Who respects or loves someone like that? So another dangerous red flag is sexual pushiness. Run, don't walk, from someone who is pushing you for what should be saved for marriage.

Dishonest

Dishonesty, lying, is a bad trait. It's not only sinful, it's destructive. You can never truly trust a liar. So if you have an inkling that the one you

Hayley,

I remember going out with this guy in college. I thought he was so cute and so cool. But one day he said something totally mean about my weight, and I felt awful. When he walked away, my best friend said, "Do you ever notice that you feel bad whenever you've spent time with him?" I had totally missed it, but it was true. I always felt worse after spending time with him, so why was I dating him? Crazy, stupid love. I quit chasing after him when I finally figured out he wasn't good for me, but it took some time and some help from a good friend to see it.

Some Signs Your Crush Could Be Dishonest

They lied for you. If someone is willing to lie *for* you they are willing to lie *to* you.

You caught them in a big lie. If they've lied to you once then chances are they've lied to you other times but you just didn't catch them. And if they haven't lied in the past, chances are they'll lie again very soon.

They have a reputation for being a liar. It's hard to swallow when someone tells you the one you love is a liar, but you have to listen. They might be crazy, mean, or both, but they also might be telling the truth. So check it out before you end up on the other end of a lie.

You have a hunch they are lying. This one is a little less red than the others (yellow flags, anyone?), but if you have a hunch they are lying it's worth finding out. The trouble with this one is that jealousy or distrust can really play with your mind, and if you are prone to thinking everyone is out to get you, then you might be seeing things when it comes to lies. Don't overreact to every little thing and start accusing your crush of lying. Try to find out quickly and quietly if your hunch is right, and if it is then break it off. Don't get overly dramatic; just walk away.

are after is a liar, it's time to move on. Liars always ultimately destroy relationships. Their inability to be transparent and honest puts some major wedges between two people. They might not have lied to you yet, but if they are liars, then you're looking at a serious red flag.

Argumentative

Some people just love to argue, and it can be cute if you're watching some romantic comedy where the anger and the sparks fly for a couple who ends up falling in love. But in reality, argumentative people, people who never seem to agree with you, are very energy depleting. They take all that good energy out of you and leave you with nothing but exhaustion. So even though you might really, really like them, you need to look ahead and think about how a life of arguing would feel to you. Do you want to live with that twenty-four hours a day? People who argue with you incessantly are not bringing out the best in you.

They Don't Share Your Faith

It can be fun and exciting to date someone who has a different faith than you, or even no faith at all. You might have a real passion for reaching the lost and so you think *Why not date them so I can help convert them?* But if a person isn't of the same faith as you then you are looking at one of the biggest red flags around. So big in fact, that God has a command against it just for you. (Check out 2 Corinthians 6:14-16.) Dating a non-believer is the biggest red flag of all. And if you ignore the flag and imagine that you can change the color of it you're lying to yourself and to God. If this red flag is flying then it's time to get out. Leave the saving to Jesus and do what he commands; don't pretend like it's okay to date a non-believer. - - -

Disinterested

Another bad and really kinda obvious red flag is disinterest. It can be kinda fun and exciting to date someone who seems disinterested. There is a thrill

Hayley,

Ugh, been there, done that. I once dated a guy who was of a different faith than me. I knew I could never marry him, but I wanted to see if things could change and he could become a believer. So I dated him even though I knew I shouldn't. I really fell hard for him, but of course, he never became a Christian and so I had to end it. It was super hard because I liked him a lot, I just couldn't marry him so why keep up the charade? Poor guy never truly understood why I ended a good thing. I didn't do either of us a favor by dating him.

to the chase trying to get them to fit you into their busy schedule or to feel more for you than they do, but dating someone who is disinterested is living in a fantasy world. If the other person doesn't show you any interest that means they aren't interested. No one who likes someone is too busy to see them. If they like you they will make plenty of time to be with you. That's how love works, it wants to be with the object of its affection. So look out for the red flag of disinterest. Don't waste your time and make yourself look like an afterthought; remember you are a temple of the living God. Not a passing fancy for a disinterested passerby.

Sexually Active

This seems like such an obvious flag that it doesn't need to be listed, but lots of people talk about loving someone who just won't settle down. They want to date all kinds of people, and so the red flag needs to go up. Did they sleep with their last three crushes? Are they still? This is a huge red flag because the more people date around, the more sexually risky situations they get into. If you see a pattern of sexual activity in someone you want to date, then don't ignore the red waving in front of your face. If they've done it with others, they're gonna wanna do it with you, it's only a matter of time. Don't become another notch on their belt.

Drugs, Drinking, Etc.

It's a definite red flag if your crush has a problem with mood-altering substances. If the one you want to spend your time with is breaking the law or just being plain stupid by drinking too much, then you can't say you didn't see any red flags when people ask you why your life went downhill so fast. Pleading ignorance to such things is not only no defense, it's ungodly. Don't partner with someone who is defying your God in this way, when you do, all you do is reject God by accepting their sin. "Stop forming inappropriate relationships with unbelievers. Can right and wrong be partners? Can light have anything in common with darkness?" (2 Cor. 6:14).

Your Parents Don't Like Them

Yup, this is a red flag. Your parents know you very well, and chances are they love you more than anybody. So if they don't like who you are dating, then you have to consider that a major red flag. Find out their objections then check them out on your own. Don't close your eyes to what they are pointing out; that just makes you a buffoon. Most of the time you are too close to a situation to really see all that's going on. You've got to trust the mostly objective but loving eyes of your friends and family to help you see what you might have been avoiding.

"Gorlock no like Michael."

So that's a few red flags that you have to keep an eye out for. They should be pretty obvious to spot, but some people might take some time believing what they are seeing. Now let's just take a look at a few yellow flags that aren't quite red but should be a signal that you need to slow down because a red flag could soon be coming.

Some Yellow Flags

Here is a list of yellow flags. When you see red in road signs and traffic signals, you have to stop and survey the situation. When you see yellow, it means that stopping isn't required, but slowing down and being more careful is definitely in your best interest. They use all kinds of yellow in road signs and signals because yellow is really easy to spot, but the yellow flags you see in your bf/gf might not be so obvious. But you have to look for yellow flags and think about them as yellow lights saying, "slow down, dangerous corner ahead." Yellow flags aren't as drastic or dangerous as red flags, but they still need to be noticed and thought about. So here are some yellow flags you might run into when you are dating.

Past Baggage

Most people have lived a little before they start to date. And depending on how much they have "lived" they may or may not have a load of baggage they are carrying along with them. Baggage in a person's life is stuff they've done, choices they've made, or experiences they've lived through that have given them some added trauma in their life. The baggage itself might not be bad, like a child from a previous relationship (the child isn't bad, the actions leading to the child were), but it can change the dynamics of your relationship. Some other baggage, like a past relationship that won't go away, drug abuse, money problems, anger, is not only heavy on the relationship but can be destructive to the life of your new love as well. If your crush has baggage of any kind that they are bringing from their past, you have to face the fact that their baggage can easily become your baggage as soon as you start dating them. So **B4UD8** it's super important to consider the person's baggage and decide if it's something you want to make your own. You'll have to start to live with the consequences of their past mistakes, and your life is gonna change because of it.

Irritating

If the person you are dating is just mildly to highly irritating, it might be a good time to rethink the whole shebang. Life is short, so why spend it with someone who grates on your nerves? This isn't the last person on earth, there are other fish in the sea. If you don't see the "irritatingness" getting better, if they don't seem willing to grow and change, and if the irritation isn't making you a better person, like iron sharpening iron, then this flag might not only mean slow down but get out.

Huge red flag!
TP should really be dispensed
over not under.

Money or Debt Problems

If you are dating someone with the idea of one day marrying them, then how they handle their money should be very important to you, because one day they'll be handling your money. Lots of people mess up with their finances but turn things around. This is a yellow flag because people can fix money problems, but it's still a good idea to slow down and make sure they aren't still stuck in money trauma. People who can't manage their money can't control themselves, and so money problems are just a sign of bigger problems under the surface. Do yourself a favor and pick healthy people to spend your time with, and that includes people with the maturity to handle money.

Secretive

We don't think that people who are dating should tell each other everything, but they also shouldn't be overly secretive and acting like they can't trust you. When people are secretive it usually means they have something to hide. But a godly person has nothing to hide. Things kept in secret are usually things that, if they got out, would be bad news for the person, and that's why they keep them hidden. This is a yellow instead of red flag because some people might just be shy or slow to reveal themselves and so there is no hidden scandalous secret. So don't see this yellow flag and run off, but find out more about them, slow down, and promise yourself you'll be honest with yourself and really look at the situation to see if it's a bad scenario or just a bashful one.

Cultural Differences

The world isn't as big as it used to be. People move all over the globe. The Internet makes it so you can meet anyone in any country in the world. You no longer live in a country where everyone is the same; it's definitely the melting pot you heard about in grade school. That means there is a chance that you are going to date someone from a different culture or region one day. And that can be kind of exciting. They are so mysterious and unique and you enjoy learning about their culture. But cultural differences can also be yellow flags. When two people come from such different cultures they can look at life much differently, and that can cause all kinds of trauma. Different worldviews, political ideas, and even social ideas can make for some added pain to your dating life. The person you're dating may be a Christian, but their family may be Hindi, and that very possibly may mean that family will reject you and your relationship. If you're both still in high school, parental objection becomes a red flag in this scenario. If you're both adults, Christians, and your crush's family is objecting because of religious and cultural differences, it becomes a yellow flag. A deep, reddish yellow. Because entering into a dating relationship of this type means great upheaval in both of your lives. If there are cultural differences between you and your date, don't run off, but definitely take things slow. Check them out and decide if you (and your families) can live with the different cultures you will be sharing with each other.

Family Flags

When you marry a person, you marry their whole family. If there is a yellow flag in their family then you've got to check things out. If their parents don't like you, if a parent is in jail, if their siblings are mean, or if they have kids who resent you, then you've got some yellow

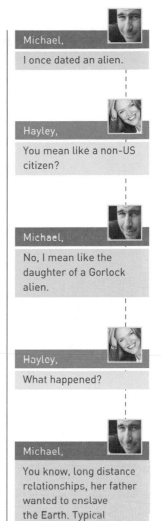

Michael,
I once dated an alien.

Hayley,
You mean like a non-US citizen?

Michael,
No, I mean like the daughter of a Gorlock alien.

Hayley,
What happened?

Michael,
You know, long distance relationships, her father wanted to enslave the Earth. Typical relationship stuff.

flags to overcome. Family issues can consume you. They don't always go away, and so if you see this yellow flag, think long and hard about how you would live with it if you were to marry into their family.

Yellow flags aren't as dangerous as red flags, but don't be a dork and ruin your chance for happiness by ignoring yellow flags just because they don't seem too bad. Give them some thought. Check them out and at least slow things down. It won't ruin the relationship if it's a good relationship. It will only make it better. So **B4UD8** promise to keep your eyes open and your mind too.

Ways to Spot Red Flags

Okay, so we've seen a few flags, and hopefully you are getting the picture. Now, it might help you out to think about how you are going to see the flags in your crush.

Family and Friends

Like we've said before, a lot of the time you are just too close to the situation to see clearly, and that's when others can help you. Talk to them about the person you are dating, give them some ideas of what they do, say, and think and ask them if they see any red or yellow flags. They can be much more objective than you can be. But just be sure that you don't get mad at them for telling you what you've asked them to help you with.

Sometimes you might not like what you hear, but it's all for your own good.

Even if you didn't ask friends or family for their opinion, don't get upset when they offer their two cents. If you get mad at them for what they say, then that's just another red flag.

Their Ex

When people break up there is usually some bad blood between them, and so sometimes the ex doesn't have too good an opinion of them. But if their ex is so mad at them that they look you up to tell you how awful they are, either your crush is bad news or your crush dated a crazy person. Either way it should be a red or at least a yellow flag. That means it's something to keep your eye on. Most people don't change their character from relationship to relationship, so if they did something mean or stupid in the last one, they'll probably do it in this one. This means that a good way to find out the flag issues of your crush is to consider what the ex is making an effort to tell you.

You Catch Them in the Act

One of the most impactful ways to spot red flags is to catch your bf/gf in the act. Red flags aren't always hidden; sometimes they are right out there for everyone to see. That means you will see them as well as the objective people in your life. But sometimes those obvious flags are the easiest ones to ignore. Probably because the

Michael,

I can talk about both sides of this issue. If a few of my exes had their way, they probably would have tried to scare Hayley off for her protection (much of it legitimate!). But instead of trying to hide my past mistakes, I let Hayley know early on that I had made some pretty lousy choices in my life and she was welcome to see if I made changes, but I would understand if she didn't want to risk it. While guys don't really do the whole "I dated her, she's psycho, watch out" intervention with guys we don't know, I've seen the exes of girls I dated supremely more happy when they broke up, which is a pretty dark yellow flag, IMHO.

person you are dating isn't ashamed to talk about it and can therefore make a good case for why they don't think they are flags at all. But just because they argue their case doesn't mean the flag is gone. You still have to take a flag for what it is, a warning sign.

By Observation

Your bf/gf might never do anything flag-worthy to you, but what about to someone else? Let's say you are out to a nice dinner and your otherwise nice date suddenly starts treating the server like a servant. Ordering them around, belittling them, or just ignoring them like some kind of slave. How your crush treats other people can tell you a lot about how they're gonna treat you once they think they've gotten used to you. Remember, everyone is on their best behavior when they are first dating; it's only after they think they are a shoe-in that their true colors can start coming out. So watch them with other people, especially when they don't know you're watching, and learn. If you see some flags, then slow the boat down and reconsider the road you're on.

Hayley,
Um, boats don't go on roads . . .

Michael,
Shush! We're on a roll.

Hayley,
A rolling wave of road?

Michael,
Now you're talking!

What to Do When You See a Red Flag

Okay, so you've spotted some red flags, what do you do now? Your first reaction might be to run far and run fast. But that reaction might be a little too extreme. Maybe you didn't see the flag well enough or maybe they just had a bad day. So take some time to find out more. Time doesn't have to be weeks or even days, but dig deeper. Find out where the flag comes from or if you even saw a flag at all. If you dig a little more, and your hunch is you've seen a flag and you don't like it, then let them know you just don't want to date them and be on your way. You don't have to give an explanation for why you don't like someone. Just say you had fun but there isn't a spark, sorry. And be done with the drama.

If you aren't so sure if it's a real flag or just your own fears or worries, then give it some time. Watch them and see if they prove you wrong. Ask people you trust to help you be on the lookout. Don't do this alone, it's too hard when you are close to the situation. So get some backup, and take the time to find out if you are seeing correctly.

Finally, if you are sure you've seen a red flag, then get up and move on. Don't ignore the red flag and hope it will go away, because if it's truly a read flag, it is signaling danger up ahead. Don't ignore the warnings!

B4Ugo

Now that you've taken a look at flag issues and gotten these thoughts into your head, don't turn back. Don't forget what you've read and ignore the flags you see in your next crush. Start to take these things seriously and you'll help keep yourself from a world of hurt. When people ignore red flags it's like watching an actor in a scary movie walk into a room where they heard a loud noise. You scream at the screen, "Don't go in there!

Didn't you hear that noise?" From the outside in, it looks like craziness to have a red flag waving in front of you and to proceed anyway. So don't be a dunce and don't let the flags flying in front of your face wave in vain.

Working Through It

If you are dating someone right now, write down all the potential red or yellow flags you see in them. Then share that list with your family or a close friend who you trust. Ask them to watch with you and check you on things as the relationship progresses.

Make a list of the red and yellow flags you would never live with:

If there are any from the list at the beginning of this chapter that you think you can live with then ask yourself why. Then talk to someone you trust about why you think you could live with that particular flag. **B4UD8** you have to be prepared for these flag issues. If you wait till you are in the thick of things, it's gonna be harder to be prepared.

Are there any flags in *your* life that others might be afraid of? Make a list.

Now think about how you can fix those flags. What can you do to move past them and re-move them so you won't miss out on that right person?

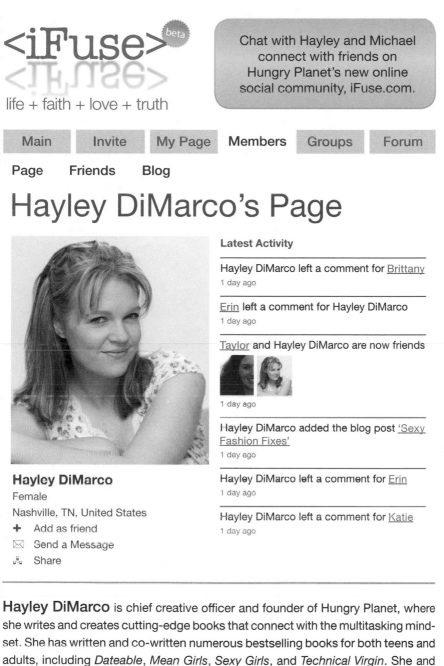

Chat with Hayley and Michael connect with friends on Hungry Planet's new online social community, iFuse.com.

Hayley DiMarco's Page

Latest Activity

Hayley DiMarco left a comment for Brittany
1 day ago

Erin left a comment for Hayley DiMarco
1 day ago

Taylor and Hayley DiMarco are now friends

1 day ago

Hayley DiMarco added the blog post 'Sexy Fashion Fixes'
1 day ago

Hayley DiMarco left a comment for Erin
1 day ago

Hayley DiMarco left a comment for Katie
1 day ago

Hayley DiMarco
Female
Nashville, TN, United States
+ Add as friend
✉ Send a Message
⁂ Share

Hayley DiMarco is chief creative officer and founder of Hungry Planet, where she writes and creates cutting-edge books that connect with the multitasking mindset. She has written and co-written numerous bestselling books for both teens and adults, including *Dateable*, *Mean Girls*, *Sexy Girls*, and *Technical Virgin*. She and her husband, Michael, live in Nashville, Tennessee.

Q4U | *from B4UD8.com*

His Parents Hate Me

I'm dating a guy right now, and it's really hard because his parents hate me. They don't want us dating, and whenever I call him they are mean and they even pretend like he's not there when I know he is. I love him so much, but it's hard to be with him when his parents are like this. I've prayed about it, but I'm not sure what God wants me to do. Can you help me understand how to make them like me?

Kendra

Dear Kendra,

Wow, this is a rough situation. We know it can feel like you are Juliet and he is Romeo sometimes, and that kind of forbidden love can be exciting, but it can make dating difficult if not impossible when parents disapprove. It's hard to say why his parents don't like you or don't want you dating their son. It might not be about you at all but about him. Maybe they think he's too young or immature to date *anybody*. Maybe they have a rule about not dating till he's out of school. But whatever it is, they have definitely made their feelings known.

From your Q, it sounds like you are asking how to look at this situation through God's eyes. If you wonder what God's will is, all you have to do is to look into his Word. Though there isn't a verse about the situation of dating someone whose parents don't want you to date him, there is a verse on parents in general, and this is how it goes: "Honor your father and your mother, so that you may live for a long time in the land the LORD your God is giving you" (Exod. 20:5). These aren't your parents we are talking about, of course, but here is the thing: if you know that his parents don't want you two to date but you date him anyway, you are encouraging him to sin. It's a sin because he isn't honoring his parents. It might not be fair, they might not even be godly people, but that doesn't change God's command to honor them. The guy you are dating has to learn to obey God no matter what the circumstances. There are always unseen things at work, and you can never be sure what your and his obedience can do in the lives of his parents, but that isn't up to you to figure out. What is up to you is to obey God and to make sure you aren't helping or encouraging someone else to disobey God. All that said, it sounds like it's about time for you to confess your sin and then to repent of it. In other words, to break up. It sounds awful on the surface, but what is more awful is knowing the truth and refusing to believe it or obey it.

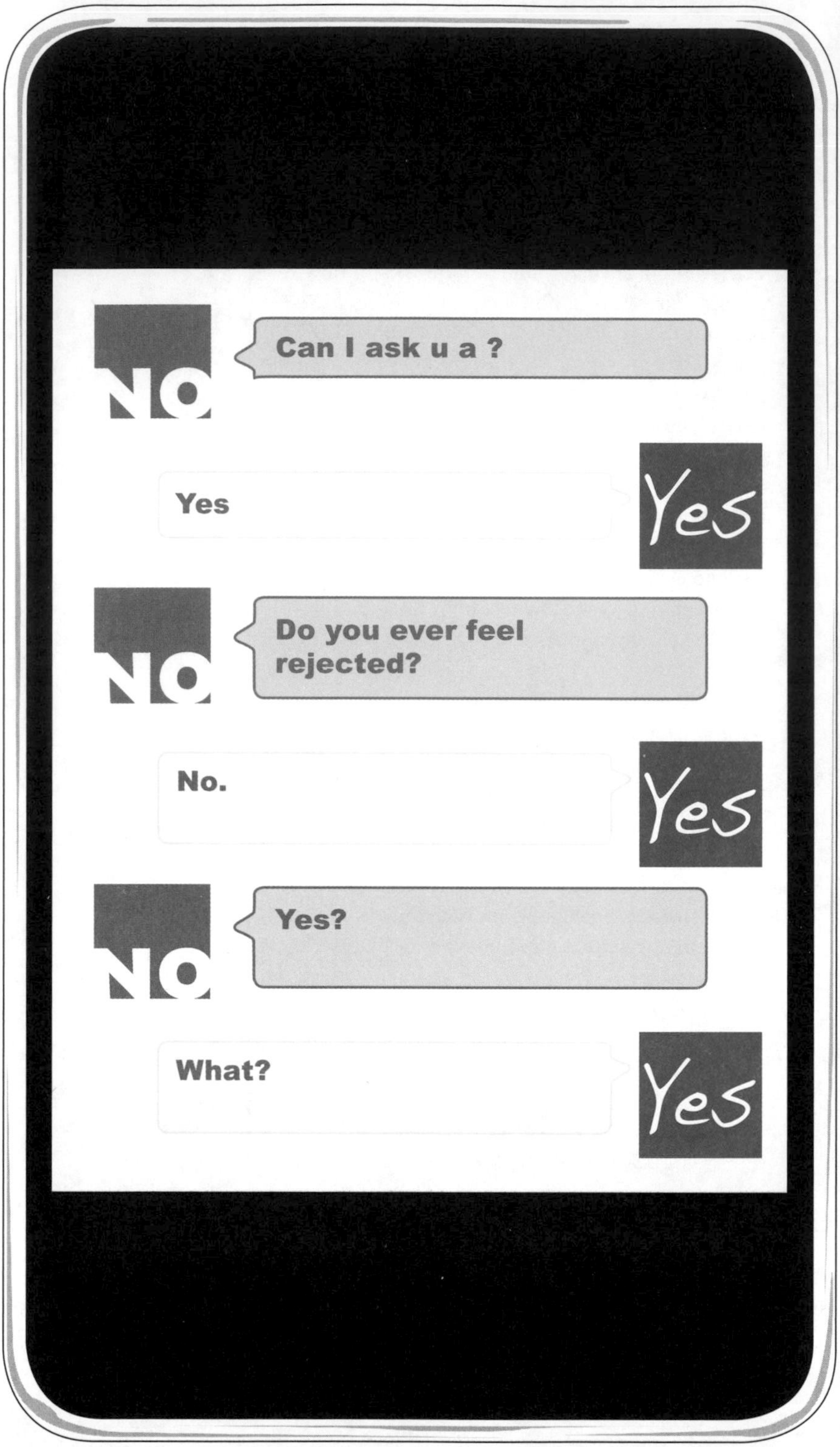
NO
Can I ask u a ?
Yes
Yes
NO
Do you ever feel rejected?
No.
Yes
NO
Yes?
What?
Yes

6: Embrace Rejection

The sixth thing you need to know **B4UD8** is how to embrace rejection. If you are fearful of rejection then that fear might keep you from doing anything where rejection is a possible outcome. And we all know how often rejection is an outcome when it comes to dating. And that's why it's important to look at rejection from the eyes of God. Here's a sneak peek: if you see rejection as a good thing and not as a horrible and fearful thing, then your dating life will show it. When you learn to embrace rejection, your whole outlook on life will change for the better. The thing you need to remember is that rejection always makes things better. Sure, it doesn't feel like it at the time. Your heart has been ripped out and stomped on (or something like it), but the truth is that will ultimately make things better. In a good relationship, you have two people who like each other. If one person is in like and the other one isn't, that's a messed-up relationship. And you don't want that, do you? Right.

So you want a relationship where both people like each other equally. That's why rejection is good; it stops the bad relationship before it starts or before it gets worse, and it resets your dating meter. You get to start over fresh without Mr. or Ms. Not Interested dragging you down and keeping you off the market. And whether you can buy that or not, at the very least can you buy the truth that God works all things together for the good of those who love him? It's true, his Word says it (Romans 8:28). If you believe God's Word then you can never fear rejection. You have to know that God's ways are bigger and smarter than your ways and he's going to make something good out of something that looks awful from your viewpoint. So learn to embrace rejection and trust God to take care of the rest. When you do you'll be more open to the people around you and less likely to set fire to a perfectly good relationship by fearing potential rejection before it even happens.

One thing to learn about rejection is that some of the most successful people in history are people who embraced rejection. They weren't successful on their first try; few are. But these successful people didn't give up. If one way didn't work, they tried another. Each one of them realized that each failure only brought them one step closer to their goal. And you can think about it like this: each time you are rejected you can know for sure that you can cross that person off your list. They are definitely not the one. And suddenly your odds of finding the one get better. So think of rejection as a necessary step on the road to success.

The Fear of Rejection

The fear of rejection is nothing new. People have been suffering from it for centuries. It's a real thing that can paralyze people and mess up relationships. But it doesn't have to be. Let's first take a look at how the fear of rejection instead of the open embrace of it can ruin or at least greatly stunt your love life.

Guys Who Never Ask

When a guy fears being rejected, his love life suffers. Why? Because he's too afraid of rejection to even ask a girl out in the first place. The truth is that most girls don't judge you when you ask and strike out. They don't dislike you any more after you ask than before. But they can get hurt and confused when you are too afraid to ask them at all. It's a compliment to a girl to get asked out. But if you are too scared to make a move, your "movelessness" tells her you aren't interested.

If you are a guy who fears rejection, then have no fear, we've got the answers for you. You can greatly improve your chances of getting a yes by doing a little groundwork. When you spend the time to read her signals and see if there is any friendly attraction at all, then you'll be more likely to get the answer you want. Girls who like you send off signals. They smile when they see you. They laugh at your jokes. They might touch your arm lightly while talking to you. If they see you seeing them seeing you from across the room then they might look away quickly in embarrassment. They also will strangely enough be where you are a lot of the time. They just want to get your attention so you can see all the signals they are sending and so you can ask them out.

Typical guy who never asks.

So here's the deal, check the signals. If you are getting some from the girl you like, then signal back. Be where she is. Smile at her. Tell her jokes.

See if she still laughs. Touch her arm lightly for a second and see how she reacts. Watch her and see if she's trying to tell you subtly that she wants you to get to know her better. If the signals are there, then embrace the chance to ask her out. Those kinds of signals greatly reduce the chances of her saying no. Now nothing removes the chance of rejection completely, and that's why it's important to understand the value of rejection. But why not hedge your bets a bit and find out subtly if she likes you. Then do the asking with courage (and a little prayer).

Girls Who Never Risk

Girls who fear rejection act a lot like guys who fear rejection. They know he won't like her, so they keep their eyes down. They don't smile in sweet hopefulness. They aren't open to his advances. They might say that they don't even care whether they are attracting guys or not. "I don't really care about how I look. You can either love me or leave me." That "love me or leave me" attitude betrays the fear of rejection, because girls who don't fear rejection risk attracting someone. They risk being where they are. They risk smiling at them, laughing with them. They make their attraction subtly known by being a girl the guy they like would be interested in.

The fear of rejection is a self-fulfilling prophecy. You fear rejection so much that you make sure you will be rejected by never being considered for rejection in the first place. The truth is that acting like you don't care at all and letting yourself go physically, avoiding eye contact, staying away from people you like, is not attractive and almost assures rejection from the get-go.

If you want to embrace rejection then you have to embrace making your presence known. If you read the section on guys who never ask then you know what guys are looking for before they ask you out. But just in case you didn't, here are some ideas.

Smile! It makes you look so much cuter.

Don't be one of the guys. Dress like a girl, because being a girl is what makes you attractive to guys. Dudes don't want to date other dudes (for the most part). So be a girl and like it.

Look at him from across the room, and when he looks back, look away quickly. That will show him you are interested. Remember, guys have more of a chance at being rejected than you do. They risk the most when they ask you out. The only thing you are risking is some subtle signs that you are interested and available.

Play with your hair while talking to him. There is something about it that's attracted men for ages, and it's a subtle signal to guys of a girl's interest. So give it a try.

Laugh at his jokes. Guys love it when you think they are funny. It tells him you don't think he's a dork. Or at least he's a funny dork.

Be where he is. He can't get to know you or ask you out if he never sees you. So make yourself available.

Touch his arm lightly. As you are talking with him, reach over and touch his arm. That breaks a barrier and gives him a signal that he doesn't repulse you.

There are lots of ways for you to risk being seen without risking rejection. You don't have to fear rejection when you work to help a guy know you are interested. In the end, if he isn't interested then he won't give you the time of day and you can move on. No harm, no foul. Just embrace the possibility that he won't like you so that you can find out if he does like you.

Obsession

One of the reasons people obsess over their crush is that they fear rejection. They fear it so bad that they spend all their time thinking about how to make sure they won't leave them. They plot, they plan, they daydream, they stalk! And in the end they go crazy with obsessing over something that hasn't even happened yet. When you embrace rejection you are actually learning to chill. And that can be a very attractive and healthy quality. If this person isn't for you, then big whoop. God has it all worked out, all you have to do is live for him. Obsession, as we've already seen, is dangerous for your relationship and your soul. So don't let the fear of rejection be your stumbling block. Embrace rejection and say to it, "You can't hurt me. I've got God on my side." When you do that, you relax and hope returns. Your face becomes brighter, your tone more confident, and your heart happier. People will find you much easier to be with and to stay with when you learn to embrace rejection.

Jealousy, Envy, Bitterness, Fear, and Even Anger

All of these could be attributed to the fear of rejection. When you fear losing what you have or what you want, your mind comes up with all kinds of ways of protecting itself. And out of that comes envy, jealousy, greed, bitterness, fear, and anger. If you are dealing with any of those, then you've got to stop fearing rejection and learn to embrace it. None of those emotions or actions are holy; in fact, they are all sinful if allowed to rule your mind and body. At the first sign of any of them, you have to stop. Stop the emotion and replace it with hope, hope that even if you are rejected it's for the best. Though for a time it won't feel like it, in the end it will be to the glory of God if you embrace rejection.

Staying "Just Friends"

Another dangerous by-product of the fear of rejection is the phenomenon of being just friends. Take two people, one who thinks of the other as just a friend and the other who hopes for more. The one who hopes for more is so afraid of rejection that they settle for being just friends. "At least I get a part of them and they don't leave me," they reason. But being just friends with someone you really like is only putting off the inevitable. Eventually they will date someone who "takes"

Hayley,

I used to be completely scared of rejecting people. I would avoid it at all costs. So when I wanted to break up with a guy I wouldn't tell him, "I'm just not into you anymore. I want to break up." That was too scary. I would just disappear. Literally. I remember breaking up with this one guy by moving without telling him where I moved. Yuck, how cruel. And there were others. I've let guys who I knew were in love with me be my friends. We did things like celebrate all our holidays together, did everything together, as if we were a couple, because I didn't want to hurt them and tell them we shouldn't act like we were dating because we weren't. Trouble is, I hurt them even more by not pulling the Band-Aid of rejection off quickly. Drawing it out and hoping they would "get the hint" was just plain cruel. And for that I apologize.

them away from you. Eventually the rejection will come, and it will come completely. The trouble with putting it off is that you build a stronger and stronger bond with someone who isn't yours to bond with. And when that bond of "friendship" is broken by your friend falling in love with someone else, it hurts worse than if you would have stopped it much earlier. You also allow yourself to be used as a filler date or stand-in. You become someone your crush uses as a stand-in till the one they really like comes along. And that cheapens you. Not only that but it keeps you off the market until the time when your "friend" finally finds the one they really want and you're left having to pick up the pieces, grumble about wasted time, and start over.

The same thing happens when you date someone and break up with them with the words "let's just be friends" on your lips. When you accept an ex-crush as a new friend, you lie to yourself. The truth is you fear dishing out rejection so much that you will settle on friendship just to keep them from freaking out. And deep down you hope, no, you know that they'll just lose interest over time and break things clean off for you. Silly rabbit.

If you are the one who does the breaking up but you still stay friends, you are being unfair and leading the other person on. Don't fear rejecting them so much that you fail to let them go so they can heal and move on. Staying just friends only prolongs their eventual pain.

Being "just friends" with the opposite sex is a defense mechanism for the fear of rejection.

Either you are using them as a stand-in because you are afraid of being alone and lonely or you are too scared to have a hard conversation. Either way, fear is running your life, and fear is a lousy roommate.

There are a lot of stupid things that the fear of rejection can cause you to do. Don't let it cloud your mind and get you off track, away from God and his purpose for your life. Rejection can never kill you, so don't give it that kind of power. Embrace rejection **B4UD8** and you'll find the world of dating a much friendlier place.

Learning How to Embrace Rejection

So how do you do that? How do you embrace rejection now that you see how dangerous fearing it can be? Well, the first thing you do is get edumacated. Learn how to reject and how to be rejected with style. What you really suffer from is fear of the unknown. You don't know how to dish out some rejection or how to handle it when it comes your way, and so you freak. But no more freaking necessary. Here are some things to know about rejection **B4UD8**.

Preparation

The truth is that rejection rarely comes out of nowhere. There are usually advanced signals, flags if you will, that if paid attention to can really help ease the sting of rejection. Of course, rejection is never easy or fun, but if you are watching and you see a sign, it can be a lot less messy.

Michael,

Yeah, I used to be really bad at rejecting people too. I hated the idea of hurting a girl, so I thought it would be easier to do things that would make her want to break up with me. Then it was off my plate. She had to do all the work. Too bad I became a jerk in the process and hurt them more than if I would have just manned up and told them I wasn't interested in them anymore.

8 Signs Rejection Is Near

1. **Their friends are acting strange.** We tend to tell our friends what's going on in our love lives, so if his/her friends start to act weird, it might be a sign that something is up.

2. **They don't want to talk as much anymore.** On the phone they don't seem to want to talk as much as you used to. They cut the call short or don't seem to want to be on the phone with you.

3. **Where's the love?** All the nice mushy things they used to say are watered down now. No more cards and cute notes. Suddenly "I love you" is replaced with "You're a great person" or "I don't deserve you." A change in communication might be a sign that rejection is on their mind.

4. **PDA alert.** Suddenly they won't hold your hand in public. No more arms around you or kisses in the mall. A halt to all public displays of affection is a surefire sign that something is amiss.

5. **Name change.** When suddenly you are no longer the boyfriend/girlfriend but are just intro'd as "my friend" or "my bud," you know what's up. In their mind you might have already become just a friend; you just haven't gotten the memo.

6. **Fights.** If you feel like you just can't seem to do anything without it erupting into major fightage, it's a sign that something is definitely wrong. Whether it's a sign of a coming breakup or of something worse, it's not a good thing.

7. **Caught in the act.** If you catch them in a lie about where they were, who they were with, or what they were doing and they weren't planning your surprise birthday party, then watch out. This isn't a good sign for the person's character or the relationship.

8. **You can't do anything right.** If it seems like everything you do is wrong or "not how they would do it" or just plain stupid, then they could be letting you know that the end is near.

If you see one or more of these signs in your relationship, prepare to meet rejection with open arms. Preemptive strikes (breaking up with them first) are extreme. Just keep watch on your heart and start to prepare your graceful exit strategy.

Excerpted from *The Art of Rejection*

5 Things You Can Do
When Someone Is Rejecting You

1. Listen to their speech, tell them you are sorry to hear it but you understand, and then say good-bye.

2. Tell them that you are glad that they told you their feelings and you completely understand that they have to go with their gut.

3. If the only thing you want to say is going to be mean, keep your mouth shut (literally). Then nod your head, turn around, and walk out.

4. Tell them that it has been nice getting to know them, wish them luck in their search, and then turn around and leave.

5. Let them know that because of how you feel for them, you can't continue to be friends, and it would be best for you to just go your separate ways and remember each other well.

Excerpted from *The Art of Rejection*

We've already seen how assessing the situation before you actually date someone can save you a world of hurt. And how working at showing someone you are crushing **B4UD8** can help the situation as well. But what about when you are in the middle of a relationship? How can you be prepared for rejection before it actually hits?

In our popular and oh-so-edumacational book *The Art of Rejection* we talked about 8 signs that rejection is near. And so to help you out, here they are.

Not letting yourself be blindsided by rejection is always a smart idea. And the truth is that it makes life easier on not only yourself but on the other person also. And whether you feel it or not, you are called to love everyone, even those who hate you. So how much more should you love someone who's loved you but just doesn't want to date you anymore?

What to Say When Being Rejected

The moment of rejection is a crazy time. Your heart is racing, your mind is racing. You want out but you want more information. You are a wreck. That's why it's so important to be prepared. Knowing what to say and how to react can give you more confidence to embrace rejection and less reason to fear it. So here are 5 things you can do when you are being rejected.

The person rejecting you doesn't have all the answers. **B4UD8** you have to know how to embrace rejection and that means being loving and kind in your response and not allowing them to lead you on with promises of friendship or bad reports about your past together. Keep things short and take all your questions and tears to God. Loving your neighbor as yourself means letting go and not trying to hold on to what has already left your hands.

Rejecting Someone?

So there are some good things to know about being rejected. You should be prepared for rejection no matter who you are. Living a life without rejection is almost impossible. So don't fear it, embrace it. But when you embrace it you also have to know that there might be times when you are the

Hayley,

Oh, it's the most excruciating thing to watch *The Bachelor* when he walks out the bachelorette who he didn't give a rose to and she demands to know why.

Michael,

I know, it makes him totally say to himself, "Phew, at least I know I made the right decision. She's psycho." Arguing with someone about why they are breaking up with you never looks good or changes anything. They're still gonna break up with you, they're just gonna feel even more convinced they made the right choice.

10 Things *Not* to Do When Being Rejected

1. **Don't ask them what you did wrong.** Anything they say here will discourage you more. So don't go there.

2. **Don't beg them to change their mind, because they just might.** Then you are stuck in a severely dysfunctional relationship. Congratulations! You convinced someone who doesn't want you that they should hang around and delay you from meeting someone better!

3. **Don't argue with their decision.** It will only make you feel more rejected when they stick to it and will make the whole thing much more of a trauma (rhymes with drama!).

4. **Don't yell at them.** Lashing out and trying to destroy them is not the best option. It won't make you feel better, and it will make you look desperate.

5. **Don't cry like a baby.** You might not have the Art of Rejection down quite yet, so showing emotion is normal. But fight off the sobbing until you get out of there.

6. **Don't promise to get revenge on them.** This is a desperate attempt at manipulation. See #2 above.

7. **Don't remind them of all the good times you've had together.** All this will do is make you feel worse because you will be remembering all the good times that are ending.

8. **Don't tell them the list of what you think is wrong with them.** This isn't a slamfest. No matter how much you think it will help, when you leave, you will still feel just as empty.

9. **Don't run out and tell everyone what a jerk they are.** That will only make you look like the desperate jilted one. Handle yourself with grace, be cool, be calm, and have an appreciation for your freedom to find "the one." You'll look like even more of a catch.

10. **Don't act like they have destroyed you, because they haven't.** They haven't even hurt you. We know, that doesn't seem true, but the pain is there because your expectations did not match up with reality. The only way you will be destroyed is if you let yourself be destroyed. It isn't what happens to you in life but what you think about it and how you react to it that matters.

Excerpted from *The Art of Rejection*

Hayley,

I remember a particular ex-boyfriend of mine begging and pleading with me not to date this other guy I was interested in. He was certain we should be together and that I shouldn't be with any other guy. In fact, he was sure that God wanted us to be together. Which seemed strange to me because God hadn't let me know about that decision. My ex just made himself look desperate and drove me away from him even further.

Michael,

In fairness to this other guy, I've been there too. Love has a way of blinding you to the point that you convince yourself there is no better option; no other option. I never did the "God told me" thing, but I've definitely done the desperate plea thing. Looking back, it's sorta embarrassing and doesn't show any confidence or trust that God's got your back in life and love no matter what.

one doing the rejecting. And for some of us that can be even harder than being rejected. So let's look at what you need to know about rejecting so you can do it with love and kindness.

Why Reject Someone?

The first thing to think about is why you would reject someone. There are all kinds of reasons you might have. Some are good and some are stupid. (We've done mainly stupid. You?) The truth is it's up to you who you reject as a date and who you accept. Since dating is such an intimate thing (potentially bringing two people together forever) it's important that you be very clear about who you accept and who you reject.

You don't really have to have a reason other than you just don't feel like dating someone anymore. You don't need red flags to pull the plug. It's your life, your choice. Even though any reason is a good enough reason, we'll still take you through some more definite deal breakers and tell you how to deliver your big bombshell while doing the least amount of damage. If you want to see some examples of why others break up, check out this list:

Abuse—This one seems like a no-brainer, but for some reason it isn't. You think that it's your fault, and you want to fix it. You think that things will get better if you just do better. But that isn't true. Abuse is never okay. Never, never, no matter what you've done, it's never okay. So if you are in a relationship that is abusive physically or emotionally, you are in the wrong re-lationship. Get out now! Did we mention it's NEVER okay?

Destruction—Two people can destroy each other in ways other than abuse. If you find that your spirit is weakening, your heart is breaking, and you don't know why, then maybe you are in a destructive relationship. If you can't say that this person makes you better emotionally, mentally, and spiritually, you need to think about changing the situation. Relationships should make you both better, not worse.

Lies—It's a sad truth, but after one of you has been caught in a lie, it's very hard to win back the trust of the other. That's why lies are so horrific; they tear away at the foundation of the relationship and mess it up, usually permanently. If you've been lied to, we guarantee you that it will take some time and effort on the other person's part to get you to trust them again. This isn't a healthy relationship. If you can't trust the other person, then you shouldn't be dating them, period.

Cheating—Don't give in on this one. If you've both decided together that you're going to be exclusive and your "someone" is will-ing to cheat on you, you can't trust them. Almost everyone thinks of physicality when they hear the word *cheat*. And if that's the case in your betrayal, we have to ask, "Were you two too physical?" If so, use this event to better reevaluate how you're getting into relationships and what you're doing when you're in them. But "cheat" can also mean an abandonment of exclusivity without telling you ahead of time. And that not only destroys your trust, it's just a sign of bad character. Better to find out now than after you're married. If someone is willing to tell you that you are the only one and then go out with someone behind your back, they don't have the kind of character that is worthy of you. And remember, it is your soon-to-be ex's fault, not the fault of the person they hooked up with.

Fights—Fights are normal. When two people spend a lot of time together, they are bound to disagree, maybe even argue, and that's okay. But if fighting is a daily occurrence, this isn't a good fit. This relationship should be the most comfortable and safe relationship you have except maybe your bff. Fights bad, getting along good.

Boredom—Be careful with this one. Boredom is a part of life, and it might be partially your fault that you are bored. But if it's obvious that there is no hope for your boredom, then walk. Don't hang on because you're hoping for some magical improvement. Boredom isn't a good sign for the future, so break it off while the breaking is easier than it will be later down the road.

Distance—If one of you is moving, it is only natural to start to think about a breakup. Dating over long distances is tough, and if you just aren't up for the loneliness, maybe breaking up is what you need to do. (Excerpted from *The Art of Rejection*.)

Trusted objection—This one is tough, but if your parents or best friends object to your bf/gf, it's not a good sign. As much as you hate to admit it, these people probably know you better than anyone. Remember, wise people seek counsel in their lives. It's smart and healthy to get the advice of the people who know you best as you drive down the bumpy road of life.

Why you break up or reject someone is really up to you. The thing is that it's important not to do too much damage while rejecting. So now let's take a look at how to reject.

How to Reject

1. Find a good location. When you reject someone it's always best not to do it in front of everyone, where they will be embarrassed. And you might not want to do it in isolation, where no one is there, in case they freak out on you. So find a good location like a restaurant, your parents' house, or a quiet library.

2. Be clear. The hardest thing to do when you are rejecting someone is to be clear and straightforward without trying to soften everything to make it easier on them. You have to be nice but you also have to be clear. Don't spend too much time explaining yourself. Get to the point and always make it about you. Don't give them a reason to argue with you. Say something like "I've really

Some Things to Say When You Want to Break Up with Someone

"I've decided that I don't want to date you anymore."

"I don't want to pursue this relationship anymore."

"This relationship doesn't feel right to me, so I have decided not to see you anymore."

"I don't see a future between us, so I'm going to stop dating you."

Excerpted from *The Art of Rejection*

appreciated getting to know you, but I just don't feel like I used to feel. And so I'm breaking up with you." It might sound too direct, but when it comes to people's hearts you have to be clear or they will think there is a way to change your mind.

3. Give them time to soak it in. After you say what you had to say, let them think about it. This is probably news to them, so don't just walk off. Expect to give them an amount of time directly proportionate to the length of your relationship. That means if you've only been dating a month or so, not too long, then keep the breakup short, like ten to fifteen minutes. But if you've been going out over a year, give them more time to talk with you, say sixty minutes.

4. Don't argue with them. They might want to argue with you to change your mind, but that's just them grasping at straws. Don't give them false hope or more grief by arguing with them. Let them

How *Not* to Break Up

Don't break up:

- in a note
- over the phone
- by telling a friend to tell them for you
- in an IM or email
- before a party you're going to together
- in front of other people
- on their birthday or any other major holiday
- on national TV (ala Jerry Springer)
- by making them so mad *they* break up with *you*
- by moving and not telling them where you moved

vent then say, "I'm not going to change my mind. I'm sorry." Then leave.

If you want to learn more about rejection than we have time to go over here, pick up *The Art of Rejection*. You'll find all kinds of info on the subtle nuances of breaking up that will help you learn to embrace rejection instead of fearing it.

B4Ugo

If you've been rejected in the past, you can't let that write your future. You were rejected by the ones who weren't made for you. So what?

Thank God! You didn't get stuck with a lemon. And your one is somewhere out there. Though rejection hurts, it can't kill you. But it can kill your love life if you decide to make rejection your identity. Don't let rejection shape who you are; let God do that. A positive, hopeful, and loving person is super attractive. A scared, bitter person is not. Don't blame your present dateless situation on your past rejections, blame yourself. It isn't really what happens to you that matters, it's only how you think about what happens to you that matters. You can either mope around in agony, looking like a sad sack who no one would want to date, or you can get up, move on, and get happy. Let rejection be a stepping stone not a trippin' stone. How you embrace or fear rejection is up to you. But what you choose will determine how well and how much you date.

Working Through It

Would you ever want to be with someone who didn't want you?

If you could learn one thing through being rejected, what would it be?

Think of five reasons why a breakup could be better than staying together.

What do you risk when you ask a girl out? (Is that so bad?)

What do you risk to show a guy you are interested? (Is that so bad?)

How many times would you suffer rejection to get to the one for you?

Q4U | *from B4UD8.com*

I don't know what to do about this boy who likes me. We are friends, and I like talking to him, he's funny but kind of weird because he acts like he really likes me. He's always hugging me and holding my hand. We talk every day on the phone and text, and last week he wrote me a really sweet poem about love. It kind of freaked me out, though, because I don't like him like that, but I don't want to hurt him. I've talked about other guys with him, hoping he would get the hint. I've even hinted about not wanting to talk to him so much, but nothing has worked. He is still acting like we are together. How can I get him to stop liking me like that without hurting him?

R

Dear R,

It sounds like it's time to break up. Sometimes breakups need to happen in relationships that you don't even consider a "relationship." When one person thinks there is something more than the other one does, something needs to be said. It's time to quit hinting and start talking. He *has* been professing his feelings for you, and by not saying anything directly about not liking him, you are leading him on. You are silently agreeing with him that you two are a thing. That's not nice and it's not holy. You've got to say something now. No matter how hard it is, if you don't do it now, it will only get harder and harder each day till you'll have to say something. And by then it will be agony for both of you. He doesn't know you don't like him, like him, and you have to tell him. It's too bad, but it's what has to happen if you want to love others as yourself.

When you do this, remember to be nice, be firm, and don't say anything about what's wrong with him, just that you want him to understand that his "love" talk and hugs and hand-holding aren't appropriate because you aren't dating, and that you don't want to date him. Tell him it's time to stop texting you and acting like you are dating, because you aren't. Make sure you don't say "let's just be friends," because that gives him hope. People believe being friends is the first step toward dating. And this guy even thinks it *is* dating. So for him, you have to just say, "I can't hang out with you anymore." You have to be direct with guys, no hints. When a guy really likes you, hinting doesn't work; they have hopes, they believe they can convince you, so no hinting, be direct.

HD: I once dated a guy who was afraid to break up with me. I could tell he didn't want to be with me anymore because he was starting to get mad at me all the time. Finally I was the one who had to break up with him. I wish he would have done it himself and saved me the heartache of having to break up with someone I didn't want to break up with. So if you want to break up with someone, do the honorable thing and just do it, don't make them do it for you.

I know I'm not supposed to date my idol, but I can't stop thinking about how popular you are and I'd really love to connect with you sometime.

i don't think so.

Am I too old? Is that it? That's it, isn't it.

7: Don't Date Your Idol

Okay, so you've had a few concepts to ponder. What's the purpose of marriage, how will you choose to take care of the temple, do you think dating is like marriage, will you keep a life for yourself, and are there any red flags you have been ignoring? All of these are essential to get a grip **B4UD8**. Now it's time to talk about idols.

Who's your idol? If you could date anyone in the world, who would it be? Now think of dating them. How would you feel? What would you do with them, for them? What would you do to keep them? If they were kind of mean and bossy, would you put up with it just to keep them around? When you think of dating your idol, you are really thinking of dating the perfect person. At least that is the fantasy. But dating your idol isn't all it's cracked up to be. In fact, dating your idol can become the fast road to your destruction.

Before we dive in here, let's just answer a few questions:

Do you think you have an idol?

Who is/are they?

Is there any chance you might be able to date them one day?

Have you been working on that?

Do you think it's a good idea to try to date that idol?

What do you think it would be like to date your idol?

B4UD8 you've got to understand why it's a bad idea to date your idol. Okay, not that you're gonna get a chance EVER to date some idol movie star or music star you love, but your idol, that perfect one, the one for you, can be a total disaster if you don't look out. Check it.

What Is an Idol?

Idols were all the rage in biblical times. People carved little creatures out of wood or cast 'em out of gold and worshipped them. Freaky stuff. Who does that? It seems so bizarre, but the truth is that there are more idols around today than there were back then; they just look different. In fact, you probably have a couple in your life right now. An idol is anything or anyone to whom you have *an immoderate (or excessive) attachment or devotion* (reference: Webster's dictionary). Sound familiar? Can you think of any idols right off hand? Hopefully not, but chances are idols aren't as hard to find as you might have thought. Here's a way to find out if you are dating your idol. Are they your obsession? Do you think about them a ton? Like, maybe even too much, like all the time? An obsession is something or someone that haunts or preoccupies your mind. Ever experience that? If you obsess about anyone, then you've made them your idol. Pretty straightforward, huh?

A person who is dating their idol will:

Do anything for them at all, even if it is illegal or sinful.

Spend hours of their life thinking about or doing something for their bf/gf when they are supposed to be doing something else.

Skip out on plans with friends and loved ones, church or other commitments in order to be with the one they love.

Give up time with God to spend time with their idol.

Turn their back on friends and family if it means keeping their idol in their lives.

Lie, cheat, or steal for their idol.

Starve themselves for love.

Destroy themselves if they can't get access to their crush.

Hurt others who hurt their bf/gf.

Hurt anyone who tries to steal their idol.

Do any of these sound familiar? Do you look like Gollum from *The Lord of the Rings* when anyone flirts with "your precious"? Then you might just be dating your idol. If someone is your obsession then the "here's the idol" sign is flashing over their head. Look out. "But what's the big deal about dating your idol?" you ask. "It's worked out good for Katie Holmes. Why can't I be so lucky?" (Um, let's not go there . . .) What's the big deal about idols anyway? Well, glad you asked.

Here's the thing: an excessive devotion to anything other than God is idolatry. Okay, so what's the big whoop about idolatry? It seems like such an archaic term anyway. How can it possibly be of importance in today's day and age?

Let's do a little study and see if we can't clear things up to figure out if idols are a big deal today or not. First let's define idolatry from a biblical perspective. The Ten Commandments start out with what important topic? Check it out.

> I am the LORD your God, who brought you out of slavery in Egypt. Never have any other god.
>
> Exodus 20:2–3

a. Who is speaking in this verse?

_____

b. Who is he speaking to? _____

c. What one term is the last sentence talking about? _____

Answer Key: a – God, b – me, c – idols

The second commandment goes on to clear this idea up. Just in case you couldn't fill in all the blanks (or read upside-down) maybe this will help. Here's how commandment number two goes:

> Never make your own carved idols or statues that represent any creature in the sky, on the earth, or in the water. Never worship them or serve them, because I, the LORD your God, am a God who does not tolerate rivals.
>
> Exodus 20:4

a. What does God not tolerate?

_____

b. What is a rival? _____

_____

So <u>an idol is anything that is a rival to God</u>. And a rival is anything or anyone who is in competition with or striving to be equal to God. Sounds simple enough. But again you say, "What does this have to do with who I date? I'm not replacing God with this person." Okay, sounds sane enough, but maybe you're not quite getting it. Let's just see if we can't clear things up by taking a quick peek at what a rival to God might do for you, k? A rival to God is someone who is in competition with him, someone who is fulfilling the same needs or job as him. Someone who serves you as well as God or that could meet your needs as good as or better than him, at least so you think. That would mean a rival, or an idol, would be someone who might do any of this stuff:

Make you feel better
Give you approval
Meet all your needs
Forgive you
Give you hope
Save you
Rescue you
Protect you
Accept you
Heal you
Complete you

Condemn you

Relieve your distress

Tell you what to do to be happy

Demand your undying allegiance

Distract you from spending time with God

Occupy all your thoughts

Hmm, know anyone like that? Maybe looking for someone like that? Sounds dreamy when you look at it like a sixteen-year-old at a chick flick. The perfect person. Or is it? Remember where we were going when we started this list? This stuff is the stuff God does. He fulfills all these needs in you. Now that doesn't mean he doesn't send people into your life to help you and comfort you, but if there is one person who is all of these, or at least most of these things to you, then you better check yourself; you might have a major rival to God. And as the verse goes, God will tolerate no rivals!

No matter how great this sounds in a person, the truth is that no human being can be all these things to you. And if they are today, then it can be guaranteed that one day they will let you down. Why? Because they are only human and they weren't made to be your everything, your god. Making them an idol is putting too much pressure on the person and the relationship. And it's a dangerous game to play with your soul.

> For of this you can be sure: No immoral, impure or greedy person—such a man is an idolater—has any inheritance in the kingdom of Christ and of God.
>
> Ephesians 5:5 NLT

Henry Martyn was born in Cornwall, England, in 1781. His father was a well-to-do businessman, and Henry grew up amid comforts. He proved intelligent, excelled in school, and went on to Cambridge, graduating with honors in mathematics. The writings of missionary David Brainerd helped bring Martyn to Christian surrender, and he soon contemplated foreign missions. "Let me forget the world," he said, "and be swallowed up in a desire to glorify God."

But he couldn't forget Lydia Grenfell. Henry was deeply in love with Lydia, though she had no desire for Asian missionary service. A vicious war tore the young man apart. Should he go to India with God, or remain in England with Lydia? He awakened throughout the night, his mind full of Lydia. He called her his "beloved idol." But, determined to do God's will, he said a final good-bye and set sail.

At daybreak on May 16, 1805, Martyn went ashore at Calcutta and was met by William Carey, who soon nudged him into translation work. Martyn lost himself in ministry, preaching, establishing schools, and translating the Bible into three Asian languages. All the while he brooded over Lydia. On July 30, 1806, after much deliberation, he wrote, proposing marriage. Letters traveled slowly, and a year passed before he received a reply. Lydia's rejection hit the young man like a thunderbolt, and his health, always frail, began to falter. He wrote asking her to reconsider. She would not, though she agreed to correspond friend-to-friend.

In 1810, his Hindustani New Testament ready for the printer, Martyn traveled to Persia hoping to recover his health. By 1812 he had grown so weak that an overland trip to England seemed the only solution. It would also, he knew, bring him to Lydia. He set out but didn't make it, dying en route at age 31. When his journal was opened, the name Lydia, like the droning of sad music, was found on almost every page.

(Morgan, Robert J., *On This Day : 265 Amazing and Inspiring Stories About Saints, Martyrs & Heroes* [Nashville: Thomas Nelson Publishers, 2000], S. May 16.)

Did you catch that? According to Ephesians 5:5, people with idols have no inheritance in the kingdom of Christ and of God. If that's not enough to convince you to avoid idols, I'm not sure what is. Idolatry can mess with your relationship with God and your relationship with the idol. So it's all around a really bad, bad idea. So why do you think it's so common? Why are there so many obsessions when it comes to love? There must be something about us as humans that helps us to obsess and to lose track of God as the right guy for the throne of our hearts.

Obsession. Allowing a person to become your idol will get you off course or tragically distract you from your real purpose in life. You can't let a guy or girl become so important to you that you leave God's call on your life in the dust.

How Love Destroys Its Idol

Who is the most perfect person ever? In fact, who is the only perfect person ever? If you didn't say Jesus, then we've got some work to do. Every Christian ought to realize that no one has ever lived a sinless life on this earth but Jesus. He was completely perfect. No sin in him, and that's how come he was the only sacrifice needed for everyone's sins. That's Gospel 101, and we assume you get that. So living on that assumption, ask yourself who else other than the perfect person could ever truly fulfill the job of an idol, an obsession? After all, an idol is something or someone you go to to fix you, make you feel better, happier, healthier, etc. There's a lot of weight on the shoulders of an idol. It would take a perfect person to handle that kind of pressure. So if Jesus is the only perfect person, then what do you think such honor and obsession does to an imperfect person, like say the person you are crushing on? Do you think they might break sometimes and fail you? Any chance they might feel overwhelmed with the responsibil-

The Thirteenth Apostle—Kyle

Not many people know this, but instead of just twelve apostles that followed Jesus around, legend has it that there was a thirteenth named Kyle. Kyle was a dude who loved the ladies. In fact, some would say he was a tad obsessed. For instance, when Jesus fed the five thousand, the apostles were instructed to gather up all the leftovers. The apostle Kyle used the opportunity to cruise the 5K for chicks. When the thirteen came together with all the scraps, Kyle told the others, "Hey, I met this Samaritan chica that I'm going to hang with. Tell Jesus I'll catch up with y'all later."

OK, so maybe we made this all up, but imagine if Jesus was hanging with you and your crowd. How obsessed would you be with following him? And would your focus (or obsession) on the opposite sex be greater or lesser because you could literally walk in his footsteps?

Here's the deal: he is with you and you are called to walk in his footsteps today and every day. Whenever you start making the opposite sex and your current crush an idol to worship instead of Jesus, just remember the thirteenth apostle, Kyle. You know, the one who didn't make it into the book?

13

ity that comes along with idolatry and want out? The truth is that every relationship built on idol worship fails. No human can handle the pressure. Of course, there have been instances, sad, sad instances where humans have fancied themselves gods and so have sought the idolatry of others. But the outcome of those relationships is always abuse by the idol of their followers' adoration. Why? Because no human can handle (or deserve) the responsibility of being a rival of God.

Okay, so not only is dating your idol bad for you and your relationship with God, but it's also bad for the object of your obsession. Bad, bad, bad. And will only end in the ending of the relationship.

Michael,

Alright, boys and girls, this is what we call the review. The revizzle.

Hayley,

Got it.

Michael,

The re to the view.

Hayley,

You done?

Michael,

The Big Reviewski!

Don't Date Your Idol

Okay, have we made enough of a case for not dating your idol? Hopefully yes. So now let's find the idols in your life to make sure you aren't dating them or turning who you date into the idol you never had.

Thinking back over what you've read in this book you might start to see something familiar below. And that's because most everything we've talked about can help you avoid dating idolatry. In fact, that's the goal of this book: if you decide to date, we want to help you date in a healthy, godly way without making the terrible mistake of making an idol out of either your crush or the dating ritual itself. Some of this stuff might have hit home, some of it might have seemed way off base or not doable for you, but either way let's just talk about how each of them can help you avoid idolatry when it comes to dating.

Date with a Purpose. Of course there are all kinds of purposes for dating, depending on who you are. But if you don't want your date to become an idol, then choose to date with the purpose of finding the one you will marry. If you date with the purpose of becoming popular or to make yourself feel better then you run the risk of creating an idol, someone who is just there to serve you, to make you feel good or successful. Dating with the distinct purpose of finding someone you will marry will greatly reduce your chances of creating an idol. But, there is one warning that comes with this, and that is, if you aren't old enough to marry then you have to be careful with this purpose because then what you end up doing is finding someone that you can't really have, at least not in marriage. And then you are left with the job of trying your hardest to keep a hold of them till you are old enough to get married. And that kind of energy put into another person is idol-making energy. It's very dangerous to seek out someone you'll want at a later date and try to keep a hold of them for as long as you can. It can make you desperate and crazy.

Take Care of the Temple. One of the quickest ways to create an idol out of another person is to bond with them sexually before you are married. Sex makes two become one, and when that happens your biggest fear becomes losing your other half. When people fear losing something they have grown to love, they can easily start to obsess about it. And that can lead to idolatry. Sexual activity of any kind can be very addictive and very progressive. You want more and more each time you are together. That desire for more can become an obsession, and obsession leads to idolatry, not to mention you've put your desire for the other person above what God has asked you to abstain from. Idol City.

But caring for the temple and not allowing it to be united illegally with someone through sex will help you avoid making idols out of people. Sex isn't just physically dangerous, it can be spiritually dangerous too because of the obsession it so easily creates between two people. So save the sexual stuff for the commitment of marriage and save yourself from idolatry.

Don't Play House. As we've said, acting like you are married when you aren't married is playing with fire. And when it comes to idolatry it's a very big clue that's what has happened. Couples who play house with each other have everything out of whack, and that rush to get all the perks of marriage without the commitment feeds the idol of self. "I want it so I'm gonna do it" you say. And suddenly whatever, or whoever, you want becomes more important to you than God himself.

Playing house can also lead to asking permission and no longer making big decisions on your own. Your first guide must be God. You have to believe that his will is more important than your bf/gf. When people start to think their significant other's opinion is the most important thing in the world, they have turned them into an idol.

It's like this: if you have been praying about it and you really think you know what God wants you to do with your life, you've got to do it. But if your crush has other plans that will take them in a different direction, you can't change everything in your life just to be with them. That would be leaving your first love for your second one. Make sense? You have to put God at the top of every decision. Boyfriends and girlfriends should be down the list. Way after God, parents, and valued friendships, those whose opinions and ideas have to matter more to you. When you give up that order of things and put your little hottie at the top of the list, you get all kinds of messed up. So make your own decisions with God as your guide and save asking permission or guidance for your real spouse.

Have a Life. You've read all about it in an earlier chapter, but you probably didn't think about it from the perspective of idolatry. When you give up your life to spend all your time with your bf/gf, you're showing some major signs of idolatry. So if you want to make sure you aren't dating your idol, decide to keep your life. Do things with people other than "the one" just to prove to yourself and God that your almighty Father is "the One" and this person hasn't become an idol. Keeping a life separate from your relationship isn't just good for the relationship, it's good for your soul. So have a life and prove you aren't dating an idol.

Don't Ignore the Red Flags. You should have a good understanding of red flags now and hopefully you're ready to look at them and not past them. If there are red flags in your relationship (or pink flags getting darker) and you refuse to look at them or acknowledge them, then you are looking at an idol. If people have pointed out red flags and you have an answer for all of them, then step back and let God talk to you. Red flags are red for a reason, and if you aren't willing to find out why, you might be playing with idolatry.

Spend Time with Your First Love. If God is your first love, your most important love, then make sure that you don't just think it but you act like it. Can you imagine how weird it would be if you were dating someone and you truly loved them but you couldn't find any time to be with them at all and instead spent all your time with someone else? Creepy, huh? Your first love would start to think maybe you didn't love them at all. And God is no different. Make sure you make time with God a priority. That means no cutting your study/prayer time short to fit in more "us time." No skipping church in order to see them. You have to keep yourself occupied with God, your first love, and then every other love will fall into line. Remember, if you seek him first he'll give you the desires of your heart (Matthew 6:33). But if you seek those desires first and him second, you can be sure you won't get either. So use your head in matters of the heart. Which option makes the most sense and has the biggest payoff? Seems like that one would be the best option, no?

Working Through It

Well, there it is. We've said it all. And now it's time for you to decide for yourself who you will be and how important dating and the one you date will be in your life. We've talked about some pretty heavy stuff. Stuff like seeking wise counsel, not dating your idol, and dating with a purpose. We might have ticked you off, frustrated you, or even relaxed you a bit. Whatever it was, don't give up. Don't throw your hands up in the air and say you'll never find the one for you, because that's not true unless you choose to make it true. Dating can be hard work, but never as hard as marriage. If you want to be with one person for the rest of your life then **B4UD8** them get your life in order. Find out who you are, what you want, and who you want. Get your priorities in place and do the work now so that when you date next you'll be more prepared for success.

Before we leave, we want to invite you over to the places we hang and talk about this stuff. Shocker of shockers, check out **B4UD8.com** for other junk related to this book. You've definitely got to check out the online dating confessional! Secondly, hop on over to **iFuse.com** if you want to hang with like-minded peeps that get things like **B4UD8**. It's an online social that strives to be idol free. Whether it's online or IRL, we hope to chat with you soon!

Q4U | *from B4UD8.com*

God Wants Me to Marry Nick Jonas

I had a dream the other night, and in it I was married to Nick Jonas. The dream was so real, and when I woke up I asked God if that was what he wanted me to do, to meet and marry Nick. I believe he does. I even talked to a friend of mine who said she had the same dream, that I was with Nick. That can't be a coincidence. I know they are coming to our town next week, and I want to get tickets so I can meet him and let him know about my dream. I wonder if he even had the same one? I'm so excited, but my parents won't let me go now. How can I fulfill God's will in my life if I can't even go to the concert?

Shayne

Dear Shayne,

Dreams can be really powerful and they can even sometimes feel like reality, but they aren't. Though God has certainly spoken to people through dreams, he never says anything in a dream that is inconsistent with his word. In other words, if you dream something that tells you to sin then you can be sure the dream wasn't from God. And if you dream something that your parents are forbidding then you know that it wasn't meant to be. Because God makes it clear in Scripture that parents are to be obeyed. And so God wouldn't give you a command to do something that your parents won't let you do.

More than likely what your dream came from was your obsession. If you spend all day thinking about the Jonas Brothers, if you listen to all their tracks and own every picture ever taken of them, if you read about them online every day and follow their TV show, then you are obsessed. And your obsessions are bound to repeat in your dreams. God never intended for anyone or anything to be your obsession other than him. So the first thing you need to do is to get rid of your obsession for this boy. You have to stop thinking about him all the time and dreaming of him and start putting God at the center of your mind. If you were really meant to be with Nick then you can be sure that God will make that happen, but only if you are being obedient and not allowing anyone to become your idol.

HD: I remember being in love with Rick Springfield, a famous singer and actor. You know that song "Jessie's Girl"? Yup, that was him. I thought he was dreamy, and so did my best friend. One day she told me that I couldn't be in love with him because she was going to marry him. I laughed and told her that was silly, I could still love him too, because I knew she wouldn't marry him. That made her so mad that she told me she could not be my friend anymore, and we never talked again. Wow, I can't believe any boy was ever that important to me, but I was very young and very naive. Now I can look back at my passion and completely understand yours. It's hard when you see someone on TV and you feel like you know them and love them. I'm just glad I didn't put all my eggs in the basket of this one star and miss out on all the real things in life God wanted to give me.

B4UD8 Gloss

Courting

Courtship is a way of dating whereby the parents of the daters are closely involved in the process, helping to determine if the two are right for each other and then being involved in the actual dating that takes place in order to insure the emotional, physical, and even financial well-being of the relationship. Courtship usually isn't agreed to by the parents unless they feel their child is ready for marriage.

Date 'n Dash

At the end of the date when the girl is being dropped off by the guy, and either the guy seems distant and detached and says good night in the car, or the girl bolts out the door of the car before the car comes to a complete stop. Then the girl gets out and walks to the door by herself. What this says to the offended party is that the date cannot end soon enough. If the guy initiates the Date 'n Dash, it also says that the guy will never protect her or care for her. It's always the best policy to turn off the car, get out, and walk her to the door. Then say good night. Is that so painful?

Dessert

Can you believe we are defining this? Of course you know what dessert is, but there are little tricks to ordering dessert on a date. Number one, always look for an opportunity to share a dessert, unless you and your date really have opposite taste in sweet stuff. Sharing a dessert allows you to connect over something sweet. If the desserts sound lame, don't be afraid to suggest getting dessert someplace else.

See Extend the Date (ETD).

Double Date

When two couples go on the same date together. The double date is a good one if you aren't sure if you are going to have anything to talk about with your first date, or if you don't really know them and you want safety in numbers.

DTR

To define the relationship. This is what happens when two people openly talk about how they feel about each other. The DTR can happen at different phases of the relationship as things progress. As the DTR happens, each of the two know they are or are not on the same page. Girls should never start the DTR conversation. When they do it is almost a certainty that they like him more than he likes her. If you're a girl and you feel like you need a DTR talk, then maybe it's time to cool things down for a bit to see what his intentions are.

Extend the Date (ETD)

When the date is going well but you only agreed to doing one thing, you can turn that one thing into two or more. For example, you both agreed to meet for coffee, but the conversation is going so well it's getting close to lunch. That's when you can casually say, "Wow, I can't believe it's almost time for lunch." Allow the other person to show interest in joining you unless your date is incredibly shy, then add a "You wanna join me?" Or you had a terrific time over dinner and you want the date to last a little bit longer, convince your date that you know of a great little ice cream place just around the corner. That way you can extend the date by taking a little stroll, instead of sitting at the same dirty table waiting for your thawed-out restaurant cheesecake.

Flowers

When giving flowers it is important to know what the flowers that you give can mean to the girl who receives them. So here's a quick rundown:

"When you care enough to say 'I just walked through your lawn.'"

Roses—Red roses usually mean "I love you," so unless that's really what you mean and you've already said it out loud, save those for later. Light roses, like pink, tend to be more for crushes. White roses usually symbolize purity and friendship. But look out for yellow, they can mean that you are overly interested! Roses are a risky first flower because of the subtle meanings they might give to different people.

Wildflowers—Guys, dandelions are not considered a good wildflower; leave them on the lawn. You can buy wildflowers at the florist or you can stop by the side of the road and pick them up, just don't pick them from her parents' front yard!

Carnations—Never, ever, ever, ever give carnations! I'm sure we'll incur the wrath of the powerful global carnation lobby, but until they spend the marketing dollars to make carnations cool again (not since the 70s) you need to avoid them.

Daffodils—Daffodils are always a safe choice. They usually represent chivalry, and what girl doesn't like a chivalrous guy. They don't say, "I'm trying too hard to get you to like me." But they do say, "I like you."

Lilacs—A very romantic flower. This is another good choice, especially if she likes purple. Totally overlooked and underrated.

Daisies—Most girls love daisies, especially the big gerbera daisies, and most would be happy to get them, but don't eliminate them by the sniff test because daisies never smell good.

Tropical Flowers—To give these, make sure that the girl who's getting them has a really flamboyant personality. Tropical flowers talk loud, so if you want to be a little less obvious and a lot more mysterious, stay away from tropical flowers on the first date.

Presentation—When buying flowers take them out of the cheesy plastic wrap before you give them to her. They always seem more romantic when they have a simple bow or nice tissue paper. Just ditch the "I bought this at the 7-Eleven" plastic wrap.

Friend Crush

Someone of the opposite sex who you like as more than a friend but you tell yourself that being "just friends" is okay. Many friendships like this end in disaster when one or the other confess their love and scare off the "friendship." If you have a friend crush that you secretly are obsessing on, then think about why you think it's okay to pretend like you are dating when you are really just a stand-in until they find someone they really like!

Friends with Benefits

When two people decide to act like they are dating but aren't actually dating. They take all the physical parts of the dating relationship and explore them but are never actually dating said friend. In this relationship both parties are using each other for physical pleasure, almost always down the road of going too far.

Going Dutch

This does not mean showing up to your date in wooden shoes or eating dinner at a fancy wind-mill. This is when you split the cost of the date. If you decide to go Dutch, for whatever reason, try to resist being a Dutch accountant where you pay for half of every activity (half of the popcorn, half of soda, half of the gas, etc.). Instead, say "You pay for dinner and I'll pay for the movie." Otherwise, you make a major part of the date managing finances, and that's not really fun or romantic.

Gone way too Dutch.

Going Steady

A term that first originated in fourth grade. The contract to go steady is usually consummated with checking a box saying you like someone, occasionally in crayon. It describes two people who like each other and have made their like known. Going steady is often time a confusing term because one can "go steady" with another and never actually do anything together. But the term does show some kind of exclusivity regardless, and because of that you can be pretty sure that when someone asks you to go steady, it means they like you.

Hanging Out

Hanging out is generally used in a couple different ways. One is "I don't like her, we're just hanging out." A lot of times it is used when describing a relationship that you really don't want to have to explain to people. "What's going on with you and Jasmine?" "Oh, nothing, we're just hanging out."

But ironically, hanging out can also mean almost dating. "We're just hanging out, seeing if we like each other." Just hanging out usually involves no romance and is just a time to find out if you like-like each other. (See Like-Like)

IDK Parrot

The I Don't Know Parrot is forever unhelpful. "What do you want to do?" "I don't know." "Where do you want to go?" "I don't know." When you do this you look like you have a brain the size of a parrot's. Be bold, be a problem solver, make a suggestion. Of course, we are going to as-

Polly want a second date?

sume that the guy comes into the date and has a plan, but circumstances can change and when the world throws your big night out a curve ball, you've got to know how to deal, and turning into an IDK Parrot just shows weakness. So help a bird out and learn to say something else more helpful, like "How about bowling?" or "Let's go to the park and swing."

Lazy Doorbell

When a guy comes to pick up a girl for a date and instead of getting out of the car and ringing the doorbell, he honks the horn. This move is not only lazy, it's stupid, because it shows the girl that she's not worth the effort and it shows her parents that you don't respect her enough to come up to the door and get her.

Like-Like

The stage of infatuation in between friends and love. As in, "Do you like him?" "No, I mean do you like-like him?" You can go out on a date with someone you just like, but you should only need one to three dates to find out if you like-like someone.

Tipping

Tipping is something you pay to service workers who earn a low hourly wage and rely on tips as their major source of income. The most common you'll encounter on a date are restaurant servers and parking attendants (aka valets). Especially when on a date, tipping is not optional. Since most of the time guys are paying, when girls see someone who doesn't tip or know how to tip, it says to them one thing: this guy doesn't know how to take care of other people, so how is he going to take care of me?

The amount that you tip is your only consideration: 15 percent is standard, 20 percent is very common if the server took good care of you. You should never tip less than 10 percent, even if the service was horrific. For parking attendants or valets, anywhere from 2–5 dollars. Never ever 1 dollar or loose change.

Valet

The guy who takes your car at the restaurant and parks it for you. When you drive up to the front door, leave the keys in and the car running. Say thank you to the guy and get your ticket, if they give tickets out. Then go in and eat. You don't tip the guy you give the car to, only tip the guy that gets your car after dinner. (see Tipping)

Virtual Dating

You are virtual dating when you say you are dating or seeing someone who you have never seen before, aka online. But you aren't really dating anyone until you actually see them. After all, the person you are chatting with might not even be who they say they are. Beware of "dating" online. If the only time you talk is online, then you are chatting, not dating.

Parent Paralysis

When you meet the parents and you don't know what to say so you end up saying nothing.

Not real impressive. To overcome your paralysis, remember that a long time ago, they were in the same situation that you are in. Always look parents in the eye and say "yes, sir" and "no, ma'am." That shows both confidence and respect.

Hayley DiMarco is founder of Hungry Planet, a company that creates cutting-edge books that connect with the multitasking mindset. Hungry Planet is where she writes, co-writes, or edits all of the company's content for teens and former teens. She has written or co-written numerous bestselling and award winning books, including *Dateable*, *Mean Girls*, *Sexy Girls*, *Technical Virgin*, and *Ask Hayley*.

Michael DiMarco is the CEO of Hungry Planet. Michael has also held positions as a Chief Marketing & Creative Strategist for *Teen Mania*, university volleyball coach, morning show DJ, and host of a humor/advice radio program called "Babble of the Sexes." Michael has co-written a number of books on relationships including *Marriable*, *The Art of Rejection*, *The Art of the First Date* and, most recently, the teen dating book *B4UD8* with his wife Hayley.

Feed Yourself Some Truth with PB&J!

The **P**ocket **B**ible study **&** **J**ournal series includes studies on

Dating
Mean
Hotness
Sex

Leading a group through the PB&J series?

Here are some great resources to get your crew excited:

- **iFuse.com**: sign up your group in the new social community from HP!
- **HungryPlanet.tv**: download videos of Hayley introducing each section of the PB & J series
- **HungryPlanet.net**: download free leaders' guides

ℛ Revell
a division of Baker Publishing Group
www.revellbooks.com

life + faith + love + truth

www.hungryplanet.net

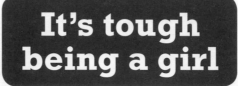